WHAT YOU NEED TO KNOW

when you can't find your UNIX system administrator

WHAT YOU NEED TO KNOW

when you can't find your UNIX system administrator

LINDA MUI

O'REILLY & ASSOCIATES, INC.
103 Morris Street, Suite A
Sebastopol, CA 95472

When You Can't Find Your UNIX System Administrator
Linda Mui

Editor: Linda Lamb

Production Editors: Ellen Siever and Clairemarie Fisher O'Leary

Printing History:

April 1995   First Edition

ISBN: 1-56592-104-6

Table of Contents

CHAPTER 3

What you need to know about running programs

You can run any command on the system by using its full pathname. Problems with commands are usually problems with the pointers to this full pathname. We describe where commands reside; command search paths; adding directories to your search path; different versions of the same command; using aliases for commands; file permissions; and how to fix problems with the TERM environment variable.

CHAPTER 4

What you need to know about sharing files

On a multiuser system, you can potentially share any file with any other user. File permissions are security measures that determine who can share what files. We discuss read/write/execute permissions; file ownership; how file owners can change permissions for a group or for the world; and what to do if you don't have permission to access a file.

CHAPTER 5

What you need to know about printing

Printing is a multi-step process; you have control over many steps in that process. We discuss how files are translated into a printer language (such as PostScript); how to test if a file is in PostScript format; how to control what printer a file goes to; how to check the print queue and move or cancel jobs; and simple printer troubleshooting.

CHAPTER 6

What you need to know about space and time

On a multiuser system, you share disk space and processing time with other users. Sooner or later, you'll need to know what to do to optimize your use of these resources. We cover how and where files are stored; checking disk space and the size of your directories; what kind of files to delete or compress if you need to create space. We also show how to deal with a slow system; how to check your processes; what processes are more resource-intensive than others, and how to kill unwanted processes.

CHAPTER 7

What you need to know about everyone else

Since you are on a multiuser system, you may need to find out what someone else is doing. We talk about using commands to see if someone on your system is logged on or has read mail; using the *finger* command to see who is on another system; creating a *.plan* or *.project* file to tell others about yourself; and finding out who is on a mail alias.

What you need to know about this book

This book is not for administrators.

This book is for UNIX users everywhere. It's for the corporate manager who needs UNIX to send email. It's for the student who has a computer account to write history papers on. It's for the physicist who needs to run a 3-D plotting program on a UNIX workstation. It's for the poor people in our production department, forced to use UNIX because it's our bread and butter.

This book is for UNIX users who are not particularly interested in computers, but who just need to get their work done. You shouldn't need to know how a combustion engine works in order to drive a car, and you shouldn't need to know how the operating system works to write a memo. But you can save a lot of calls to your auto club if you just know a few small things: how to fix a flat, how to add motor oil, how to stick a pencil in the choke of a carbureted engine, etc. The same with UNIX; you can save a lot of calls to your administrator if you just learn a few basic things.

We do assume some things about the reader.

We assume that you use a UNIX computer. We assume that you know some basic things about using UNIX, such as changing directories and editing files. If you need help with basic UNIX commands, we recommend you have another book on hand as a reference.

We assume that you aren't working by yourself, but are in an environment with other users and with an available administrator.

UNIX can wear many different hats. There are several vendors of UNIX systems, and each system has its own peculiarities. Don't be alarmed if the output of a command on your system looks slightly different from the output shown in this book. For the most part, the differences are only cosmetic. When there are serious discrepancies between different versions of UNIX, we cover both versions.

Some users may work under a graphical user environment, usually based on the X Window System. We don't cover issues involved with using X in any great detail, because there are so many different implementations of X that you may be using. Since most X users have access to a terminal emulator, we orient the book to running programs from the UNIX command line. Trying to cover X environments in this book would be like trying to write a generic book about how to program your VCR: every manufacturer does it differently, so in trying to be useful to everyone, the book would be useful to no one.

What if you use UNIX only occasionally—if you are a Macintosh or PC user who "has to" use UNIX for mail or downloading files? Although this book isn't written *for* Mac or PC users, we'll try to point out contextual stumbling blocks you might run into: how UNIX treats issues differently than the system you're used to. If you understand some of the philosophy of UNIX, you'll be able to make more sense of the parts of UNIX you need to use.

We don't assume any particular interest in UNIX, but we expect a willingness to try to figure it out. We promise not to try to make you love UNIX if you promise not to be determined to hate it.

This book has seven chapters, each ending in a quick-reference section.

This book contains seven short chapters:

- Chapter 1: What you need to know about solving problems
- Chapter 2: What you need to know about logging in
- Chapter 3: What you need to know about running programs
- Chapter 4: What you need to know about sharing files
- Chapter 5: What you need to know about printing
- Chapter 6: What you need to know about space and time
- Chapter 7: What you need to know about everyone else

Each chapter ends with a quick-reference page that summarizes procedures from the chapter.

Every UNIX computer site is different. There are procedures that depend on how your site is configured, and commands that may work slightly differently at your office. The quick reference page therefore includes a "worksheet" for you to write down site-specific information. You might get this information by asking your administrator.

Feel free to photocopy these quick reference pages for other users in your office. (That way, not everyone in the office will have to ask the same questions.)

This series puts technology in context.

Like other books we've published, the What You Need To Know series started with a need that we had for a certain kind of information. Tim (O'Reilly) noticed that we had nothing to give our new, nontechnical employees about subjects they needed to understand in order to work here productively. The kind of information our users need is not "Push this button," it's more "Here's how to think about this."

So we developed a series of books to tackle the issues encountered by people like many of us at ORA—people who use technology as a tool for their "real" job. The books digest and present the kinds of information you'd come across if you worked with the technology for a while, in a supportive and knowledgeable environment. These are books we will be handing to our own employees.

This book is designed to be browsable.

Depending on how you want to read the book, you can get your information from first-person stories, frequent headlines that tell the gist of each short section, the text itself, or reference sections. We have sidebars of users telling stories, because people learn from personal experiences. (After you've seen someone embarrass themselves company-wide by misaddressing their mail, you'll be sure to check the To: field in your own messages.) So we have users telling about their embarrassing moments and their personal ways of looking at technology. The anecdotes aren't fluff to cajole you through the material. They *are* what you need to know. By reading the stories alone, you can get the gist of the material.

Headings that summarize main points and short, standalone sections also encourage browsing. How-to sections are segregated into their own format, so that you can easily skip—or find—specific procedures.

Of course, reading straight through all the chapters is also an option. We hope that when you "dip in," you'll find so much of use that you'll keep reading.

Contact us to suggest improvements, or for sales information.

Our U.S. mail address, phone numbers, and email address are as follows:

O'Reilly & Associates, Inc.
103A Morris St.
Sebastopol, CA 95472

707-829-0515
fax 707-829-0104

UUCP: *uunet!ora.com!nuts*
Internet: *nuts@ora.com*

For information on volume discounts for bulk purchase, call O'Reilly & Associates, Inc. at 800-998-9938, or send email to *linda@ora.com* (*uunet!ora.com!linda*).

For companies requiring extensive customization of the book, source licensing terms are also available.

I'd like to thank some people...

This book is the brain child of my kind editor Linda Lamb, as part of a series of books for end-users. When I saw the proposal for *What You Need To Know When You Can't Find Your UNIX System Administrator*, I marched to my boss to say "sign me up for that!" I know it sounds implausible, but that's pretty close to how it happened.

Why was I so interested? Because it was an opportunity to write about UNIX and computing in general in language that anyone can understand. Too many of our books are written with the underlying attitude, "If you aren't interested, you should be!" They're written for people who think computers are neat and just can't get enough of them.

This is fine for most of our books, which are written for computer professionals. But whenever I help a coworker with a problem here at our office, I realize that there's this disenfranchised class of users who don't know much about computers and don't particularly care. They don't want to be power users, and they shouldn't be made to feel as if they should be.

Here's my pet peeve. Every night I watch the TV weatherman tell us what the weather was today, show us a radar map of the region, and then explain how a low-pressure system over the Rockies will be pushed up by a high-pressure system coming up from the Gulf, and so on and so on. And I become truly annoyed, because all I want to see is the five-day forecast showing the pattern of sun, snowflakes, and high temperatures for the coming week. If we're going to get some rain on Tuesday, I don't particularly care why, all I want to know is that I should carry an umbrella.

Just as most TV viewers aren't meteorologists, most UNIX users aren't computer scientists. And just as I think that TV weather forecasts should cut ahead to the five-day forecast, I can tell that most of the people I try to help with problems just want me to hurry up and get it fixed.

Now, we aren't going to write books for people who don't care at all, since they don't buy books. But this was an opportunity to write a book for people who only care as much as they have to.

Enough about me...on to the acknowledgments.

Before anyone else, I'd like to thank all the people who agreed to be interviewed and then have their faces splashed across the pages of this book. Those gallant individuals are: Jane Appleyard, Joan Callahan, Mary Jane Caswell-Stephenson, Edie Freedman, Nicole Gipson, Tanya Herlick, Paul Kleppner, Rebecca Kondos, Linda Lamb, Allen Noren, Eric Pearce, Dick Peck, Arsenio Santos, Mike Sierra, Ellen Siever, Carol Vogt, Linda Walsh, and Frank Willison.

I'd like to thank the reviewers of the book. Within O'Reilly & Associates, I'd like to thank Rebecca Kondos, Tim O'Reilly, Eric Pearce, Arsenio Santos, Ellen Siever, Norman Walsh, and Frank Willison. External to O'Reilly & Associates, I'd like to thank Dan Barrett of UMass Amherst, Peg Schaffer of Harvard University, and Pat Wilson of Dartmouth College. Also, I'd like to thank Ellie Young of Usenix for recommending reviewers for the book.

Many thanks and appreciation to those who worked on the production of this book. They include Clairemarie Fisher O'Leary, Nicole Gipson, Kismet McDonough, Kiersten Nauman, Jennifer Niederst, Nancy Priest, Mike Sierra, and Ellen Siever. I was astounded by how my random scribbles were turned into the crisp, elegant, and (of course) error-free product you hold in your hand.

Finally, I'd like to thank my patient and pleasant editor, Linda Lamb, for her inexhaustible support while I slowly plugged along. In addition to interviewing at least half our subjects, Linda was the one who maintained a clear vision of the book while I faltered. All this while working on a book of her own.

You'll notice that up until this section, I've used the first-person plural "we" in place of "I." This is because I've thought of this book as a collaboration between Linda and me, and it was only when I had to acknowledge her in the third person that I felt forced to use the singular.

CHAPTER 1

What you need to know about solving problems

There's no magic involved.

So you're in the office alone at 10PM, and there's no administrator to be found. Or you're in your office at 11 AM, and your administrator isn't responding to your email. Or you don't think your problem is important enough to bother the administrator.

Many problems that users have on UNIX systems don't really require the system administrator. A lot of the time, all you need is someone who knows the system a little better than you do. And in fact, a lot of the time that person could be you; it's just a matter of learning your way around the neighborhood.

Many users think that UNIX is some mystical land that only the technically worthy may enter. UNIX certainly tries to build itself up that way. Commands are called bizarre things like *grep* and *awk*. People *finger* and *ping* each other, and experts call themselves "gurus." A famous poster shows a conjurer stirring a swirl of potions with magical words like *perl*, *biff*, *emacs*, and *troff*. UNIX people have this annoying way of pronouncing things in unintuitive ways (such as *TeX* and *vi*), perhaps so they can tell the Outsiders from the people "in-the-know."

The truth is, there is no magic. The computer is merely a computer, and it's not that complicated. It's just that UNIX was made for the tinkerer, not for the user.

What was your first impression of UNIX?

Fear and loathing.

I now think of UNIX as having the personality of an eccentric aunt. I'm not always sure whether to be afraid or intrigued.

Rebecca Kondos

Whenever your administrator or other experienced user helps you with a problem, it always looks like unintelligible commands fly out of their fingers, and that you'll never be able to understand what they do. That's not true. Yes, experienced users know a lot of shortcuts that make their work hard to follow, but the actual skills they use are just common sense and a bit of knowledge. You probably already have a bit of the former, and the latter is pretty easy to learn once you set your mind to it.

For user problems, administrators are more like detectives than like magicians.

When users have a problem, 90 percent of the time the administrator spends on it is gathering information. After that, it's just a matter of ruling out possibilities, making theories, and tweaking things until they work.

Let's take a case: a user complains that the printer doesn't work. The administrator needs to find out what printer he was using and whether other people can use that printer. This tells the administrator whether the problem is with the physical printer.

If the printer is fine, the next thing is to find out if the user can print other files. This tells the administrator whether something is wrong with the user's configuration in general, or whether the problem is something specific to printing this particular file.

If the user's configuration is okay, next the administrator might find out how the file was created. She might then try to create another file the same way. This tells her if there's something wrong with the application that created it.

And so on. UNIX administrators go through the same process that we all do with a puzzle. We isolate the possible problem areas until we pinpoint where things went wrong.

Administrators have many responsibilities; user support is only one of them.

Although administrators need to address user problems, individual users can't always be their highest priority. Administrators need to take care of systemwide issues before they can spend time on problems that only involve a single user. For example, if the system is nearly out of space or the network connection is down, an administrator shouldn't stop working on that problem just to help a user print a memo.

Some office environments have a squad of administrators who are happy to help you with your every move. More commonly, however, offices have a handful (or fewer) of overworked administrators, whose responsibilities include:

- Maintaining hardware, including computers, terminals, printers, modems, and sometimes even the phone system
- Maintaining software, including the operating system, applications, servers, etc.
- Maintaining the network, not only the physical network, but also the configuration of servers
- Maintaining computer security
- Ordering new hardware, software, etc. (which means spending a lot of time talking with salespeople)
- Installing new hardware, software, etc.
- Doing backups
- Training users
- Problem solving

When there are multiple administrators at a single site, the administrators are likely to break up these responsibilities among each other, each becoming a "specialist" in a certain area. Think of it like health care: like the human body, computer networks are complex, and a single practitioner can't always fix a problem without consulting others with more expertise. At one site, you may have a Macintosh administrator, a PC administrator, a hardware expert, someone else who works primarily on network configurations, and someone who performs printer support. The nature of a problem may overlap

Moving to UNIX from a Mac or PC

Mac users have a steeper learning curve coming to UNIX than DOS users do.

DOS users are at least familiar with a command-line interface: putting spaces before options, piping output of commands, and a tree-like structure of files. DOS users are used to pathnames. Mac users have folders, but they don't tend to think of them in that hierarchical manner.

Mary Jane
Caswell-Stephenson

How did you feel learning UNIX?

I learned UNIX by the kindness of strangers. I learned who knew something about the system and who wouldn't growl at me if I asked.

Joan Callahan

I first encountered UNIX at Columbia University. The college computer center had literally thousands of users. There was no chance of ever finding a system administrator.

The university would hire students as consultants, who were supposedly available over email. If you sent mail to a consultant, you would either get no response or occasionally, after waiting days or weeks, an "I don't know." We were thrown back on our own resources.

Arsenio Santos

I hated UNIX when I first met it. The hardest part was knowing how to find information. And there are so many ways of doing things that you never know which is the best way.

Later on, I found I liked UNIX. But I didn't realize that I liked it until I went back to my old system and found myself saying, "Where are my directories? Where's the grep command?"

Ellen Siever

The calculator was the most complicated thing I had ever used before I came to work here. And it was one of the really simple ones—it didn't even have a cosine button. I don't program a VCR, and I don't have an answering machine. I'm the least technical person.

I had never used a computer before. Well, actually, I did. I used my friend's computer in college to type papers. But when I needed to change anything, like even to fix a typo or something, he would have to do it for me.

Now I really like UNIX. I can do things. When I have a problem now, I try to see if I can figure it out myself.

Jane Appleyard

The way I learned stuff was asking more knowledgeable people in the office. Or sometimes someone watches me do something and they say "I can't believe you do it this way," and they show me a better way to do it. I keep a notebook by my computer now with all sorts of notes about things to do. If it's in my notebook, then I feel that I know it, or at least can do it.

Nicole Gipson

several different fields—so if you have trouble printing from your PC, it may involve PC, printer, and network expertise.

There may also be an administrator dedicated to user support. If so, then you should probably look for the user support person before you consult anyone else, the same way you often have to see a primary care doctor before you make an appointment with a chiropractor.

Educated users get better help.

Your chances of getting help from your administrator are better if you know more about what's happening.

Why? Well, apart from the technical snobbery, there are also some legitimate reasons:

- Educated users are more likely to give the administrator the information needed to solve the problem quickly, without having to do a lot of detective work. If instead of saying "I can't print," you say "the *xmail* program doesn't print correctly, although I can print from other programs," you will save a lot of time for the administrator.

- Educated users are more likely to be able to act on a quick answer, such as "looks like your *.login* file is broken." For another user without much UNIX background, the administrator may have to compose email explaining what the *.login* file is, why a change to that file might cause the problem, how to fix it, etc.

- Sometimes an educated user may know exactly what the problem is and even offer the solution.

To illustrate the different responses that two users might get, compare the following two mail messages:

```
I'm having trouble editing /home/lois/updates. I use the
emacs program to edit. I typed:

% emacs updates

The error I got was:

Please set the environment variable TERM; see tset(1).

I also tried editing other files, but it didn't work for
them either.
```

Error messages

Whenever a user gets an error message, they should just cut and paste it, both the error and the command that they ran, and email it to me. That gives me the best chance of figuring it out without having to go to their office and watch over their shoulder.

Tanya Herlick
administrator

When I see error messages, I always look at them, because I've learned that when I go to someone with a problem, the first thing they ask is whether there were any error messages. So now I always go armed with my error messages.

Nicole Gipson

```
I didn't use to have any trouble. But my X terminal was
given to someone else yesterday, so I'm logging in from my
Macintosh. Is that the problem?
```

In this message, the user says what the symptom was, what she typed, and what error message she got. She also describes something that changed, which may or may not be a factor. This is a lot easier to respond to than:

```
I can't edit my files! What's going on?
```

In the second message, any number of things might be wrong. The administrator doesn't know what editor program the user uses, what files she was trying to edit, whether she used to be able to edit files, or whether something changed recently.

The first message can be solved very quickly: the administrator sees the error, interprets it, and can send off a quick message to the user explaining what to type into her *.login* file. The second message is one that the administrator can't know the answer to without more information, so it may be put on the back burner until the administrator has more time to spend on it.

Put yourself in your administrator's shoes.

When I was a system administrator, I knew that there was no substitute to sitting down with users and watching over their shoulders while the problem was recreated. By putting myself in their shoes, I could see firsthand what their goal was and what was going wrong. I could see unusual output or errors, and I could try things slightly differently. Unfortunately, I didn't always have the luxury of spending a lot of time this way.

So if your administrator can't put herself in your shoes, you can try to meet her halfway—put yourself in her shoes. What would she do? What would she ask?

Also, remember the "do unto others" adage. You don't particularly like it when people rudely barge into your office, demanding that you drop everything for them. Remember that administrators are people too, and are often under a lot of stress. Try to be patient and polite. And be considerate in how you phrase your requests—just because it's the administrator's role to fix a problem doesn't mean it was her fault the problem occurred.

What you need to know about solving problems

Gather the facts before you alert your administrator.

When you go to a tax preparer, it goes much faster if you first locate and organize all your paperwork. Similarly with administrative help—you'll get better results if you get all your facts together before you go to the administrator. Neither a tax preparer nor a system administrator can complete their work if you don't give them all the relevant information.

So before you call a system administrator, do some of the leg work yourself. It helps if you know what sorts of things your administrator will be looking for and provide that information ahead of time. Copy down the error messages and maybe try to interpret them for yourself. Think of what the obvious things are and check those things first. Try doing something a couple of different ways—if one way works and another doesn't, that will help the administrator determine where the problem lies. Write down everything you did to solve the problem and then send that in email to the administrator.

The best part is, when you're done learning what's what and assembling your information, you may discover that you don't need an expert to help you after all.

Recreate the problem.

When something goes wrong, the first thing you might do is to try to recreate the problem.

This isn't because you're hoping something miraculously changed and that the hex is lifted (although I suppose it doesn't hurt to hope). It's so you can make sure that there is really a problem. Did you mistype the command? Were there any error messages that you missed the first time around?

It's true that there are times when retyping the command may make things worse. For example, if you've lost data in an editor, opening the file again may overwrite any "backup" copies still on disk.

But if you feel secure that retyping the command can't make things any worse, try to recreate it. Once you can recreate a problem, you're one step closer to fixing it. In addition to giving you a process that you can break into components, it also gives you a way to test when the problem is solved.

Twenty questions

The most frustrating part of the job is the twenty questions. Someone tells you about a problem and you tell them to back up a bit, and you start asking them what they were doing at the time, and whether anything changed recently, and so on. And usually they walk away before the questions are done, because in answering the questions they've figured it out for themselves. If they asked themselves the questions on their own, everything would go much more smoothly.

Eric Pearce
administrator

Look at the error message.

A UNIX error message often scares users off. But a lot of the time, it makes sense if you read it carefully. Like a legal document, an error message is written in English; it just uses different words than we do in conversation.

If you can't interpret an error message yourself, then the next best thing is to copy it down for the system administrator. When you send the system administrator email, you should tell her what directory you were in, showing exactly what you typed and what error message(s) you saw.

Try the most obvious answers.

What obvious answers can you think of to check first?

For example, if the printer isn't working, are you sure it isn't out of paper? Sure, maybe you just refilled the paper tray a few minutes ago...but it only takes a second to check. Maybe someone stole paper from the printer to put in the copier.

If your password doesn't work, are you sure you're typing it correctly? Are you sure that you have a login account on this machine?

If you can't run a command, are you typing it correctly? Are you sure that the letter l you read in the command-line option isn't really a number 1 or a capital I? Are you sure the capital O isn't really the number 0 (zero)? Are you sure you ran the command from the right directory? Is there an error message that might give you a hint?

If your terminal doesn't work, is it plugged in? Is the brightness control turned all the way up?

This line of questioning may put you off. But these "obvious" problems are the first things your administrator looks for, because they are common and because most people don't bother to check.

If it used to work, what changed?

If what you're trying to do is something you've done before, then something must have changed for it to behave differently now. Sometimes it changed at the system level, in which case

Things would go more smoothly if users understood the system

Once I came into work and saw a piece of paper taped to my chair that said "email is down." That's all it said.

First I checked email, and of course email was working. To figure out what was going on, I had to go through this whole procedure where I tried to figure out what this guy might have been doing to make him think email was down.

I started by trying to see things from the user's perspective, "Okay, this guy uses a Macintosh. And he reads email through the UNIX computer." Then I realized the only thing he uses UNIX for is email, so when he says email is down, what he probably means is that he can't get into UNIX. It turned out that there was something wrong with the Macintosh gateway or something like that.

As far as the user was concerned, UNIX equaled email, so that's how he phrased his complaint. He didn't understand how the network was set up. He probably didn't even know that he was logged into another machine to read email.

A lot of users, all they learn is a memorized sequence of commands. To read email, they type "telnet rock", and then they type in their user name, and then their password, and then RETURN when it asks about the terminal type, and then "mail." Maybe they just have those commands written on a piece of paper taped to the side of their computer.

All they know is that this is how to get their email. So if any part of that process is broken, all they know is that something's wrong with email, so email must be down. When they complain to us, we can't start fixing the problem until we first translate what they say into something that makes sense.

I understand why they phrase it like that. But it creates so much more work for us. We should be doing better employee training. We show new people how to do other things for their job, but when it comes to using the computer no one tries to explain anything. So when they have any problem at all, all they know is to come running to the system administrator. And then we have to start from scratch to figure out what they were trying to do, because they don't even know the right words to use.

Eric Pearce
administrator

it's your administrator's problem. But often it's something in your own environment.

It's not always easy to remember what may have changed, but the exercise is worthwhile. Even if you don't think something is relevant, it may be. The *chmod* command you ran on your home directory files yesterday may be the reason you can't log in today. The change to your search path last week may be why the *finger* command is acting differently this morning.

If a command used to work, try to remember when you last used it, and see if you can pinpoint what may have happened in the interim.

Try to identify (and eliminate) as many factors as you can.

Detectives need to come up with suspects before they can think about motives. Similarly, you need to figure out what factors are involved before you can track down why things went wrong.

For example, when you're having trouble printing a file, there are several levels at which things may have gone wrong. Try to identify all of them:

- Is the printer working? See if there are other printouts coming out on the printer, or ask other people if they are having trouble.

- Can you send jobs to the printer using a different application or from the command line?

- Are you sure that the job is going to this printer? Do you see it on the printer queue?

- Can you print successfully to a different printer?

- Is the file you're trying to print in the correct format?

Once you have your suspects, you can start ruling out the ones with alibis. By answering these questions, you can help identify whether the problem is with the physical printer, the UNIX print spooler, your application, or your file.

For example, if others can print successfully to the printer, then you know that there is nothing physically wrong with the printer or with the system's communication to the printer. If you can send jobs from a different application or from the command line, then you know that it isn't something general about your environment, but something specific to this application. And so on.

Tell the administrator what you tried.

If in your adventures you don't solve the problem, send the administrator email describing exactly what you did—what you were trying to do, what happened instead, and the results of your investigations before you gave up. Spending an extra minute or two describing the problem in detail will pay off in a faster response from your administrator. Don't be shy about telling your administrator about guesses that were incorrect, or clues that led nowhere. Any information is better than no information at all.

If it's something you need fixed immediately, you can contact your administrator in person as well. But many administrators insist on email regardless. With email, administrators have a record of the complaint and any extra information that you may have passed on.

What can be fixed

When there is something wrong on UNIX, you don't always know. You can go a heck of a long time not knowing that this annoying thing you put up with every day can actually be fixed.

Linda Lamb

Users' perspectives: Having a problem fixed or fixing it yourself

When someone tries to fix a problem for me, I usually want to understand it. I don't like it when someone just whizzes by with a bunch of commands and everything's magic. I'd rather know how to fix it myself next time. The exception is when I'm on a deadline—the couple of days before a deadline, I don't care about anything except getting it fixed.

Ellen Siever

I've had a recurring problem with my X terminal.

The first time it happened, I called Glenn frantically. "Glenn! I'm dead!" Glenn traced the whole connection into the phone room and found that a wire had become unplugged. He plugged it back in.

The second time, a day or two later, I also called the sysadmin immediately. "Glenn, I'm dead again." Glenn found the problem more quickly this time and fixed the wire again.

The third time, I followed along when Glenn went into the phone room and watched as he jiggled and pushed at the wire.

Now I'm familiar with that old wire. If I lose my connection, I jog right into the phone room and push in number 33.

If a problem is consistent, I prefer to learn to fix it myself. It's easier. It saves me time. I don't have to hassle my sysadmin. That way, I save my requests for when it really counts.

Rebecca Kondos

When I have a problem, the first thing I do is look back in my history and see what I did, since most of the time it was something I did myself.

I'd make sure I was in the right directory.

I'd look in some books a little.

And then if I haven't figured it out by myself, I'll ask someone. Usually, when I ask, I preface it with "I'm pretty sure this isn't something I can take care of myself, so can you take a look?"

I like to see how someone else fixes the problem. And I like it when they explain how things work. If I understand how something works underneath, then the stuff on top makes more sense.

It used to be when I first started that most of the time it was something that was my fault, but lately my percentage has been going up. Now 80% of the time it's someone else's problem and 20% of the time it was something I did. When I first started, it was more like the other way around.

It makes me sort of sickly happy when it isn't something I did myself.

Nicole Gipson

What you need to know about solving problems

contacting your administrator

Include this information

When sending email or leaving a written note for your administrator, try to include the following information:

- *Describe the problem clearly.* Don't just say that a program is "acting weird," but show exactly what you typed and exactly what symptoms there were.

- *List any messages that you saw verbatim.* Copy them down or copy and paste them into email.

- *What were you doing when this happened?* Have you done anything unusual recently? Have you noticed anything else out of the ordinary?

- *Did you try anything to fix the problem?*

Where to reach your administrator

Ask your administrator for contact information:

Email addresses: _____

Aliases (if any): _____

Phone extension: _____

Beeper information: _____

_____

Specialists

At some sites, you contact a different person according to the type of problem. Identify and supply contact information for the administrators responsible for:

Printing problems: _____

_____

Network problems: _____

_____

Mail administration: _____

_____

News administration: _____

_____

General software problems: _____

_____

User support: _____

_____

CHAPTER 2

What you need to know about logging in

If you can't log in, you can't do anything else.

Not being able to log in is like losing your car keys. You can't get very far until you solve the problem at hand.

Logging in is part of your morning ritual. You enter the office, grab a cup of coffee, and then log in. For me, I find that I can only relax at work after I've logged in and read my email, sort of the same way I need to listen to my phone messages before I can relax at home. If you can't log in, you feel displaced. Your daily routine has been interrupted. You are disconnected from your work. You are helpless.

Or *are* you helpless? Even if your administrator hasn't arrived at work yet, there's some simple troubleshooting that anyone can do. Rather than sit around drinking too much coffee and rearranging your desk, you can try to fix the problem yourself.

Logging in is a series of steps; each must be successful.

When the login process is working right, you hardly notice it. When things go wrong, you need to focus on the underlying series of steps, each of which must happen before you can log in and begin work.

The necessary components for a successful login are:

- The terminal must have power to operate (i.e., must be plugged in).
- The parts of your computer that need to talk to each other (keyboard, hard drive, monitor, etc.) must be physically connected and plugged in as needed.
- The terminal on your desk must be able to communicate with the main computer through a network connection.
- You have to correctly enter your login name and password.
- The computer has to find a match for your login name and password in its password database.
- For X terminal users, the start-up files that set up your environment when you log in must work correctly.

If the terminal doesn't seem to be on, check the power supply.

Sometimes the terminal just isn't working. There is no sign that the terminal is even on. You listen closely, but you don't hear a fan whirring or any other signs of mechanical life. You turn the switch on and off a few times, to no avail. You're no expert, but you feel fairly confident that the Terminal Is Broken, period.

There's nothing more embarrassing than calling your administrator and all they do is push in your power cord. Your terminal might have been unplugged when you were moving equipment, or by cleaning people who accidentally bumped a cord.

When the computer isn't working, start by checking the simplest and most obvious things first:

- Make sure your terminal is plugged in. Most power cords for computers are detachable on both ends, so check that the cord is plugged securely into the computer as well as into the wall socket.
- Make sure you've turned on all the necessary power switches. Sometimes there are multiple power switches, for example, one on a monitor and another on a base.
- Plug a lamp or radio into the electrical outlet, to make sure that the outlet itself works.

- Sometimes a computer may have a switch to control what sort of electrical input it uses. For example, a computer may be designed to toggle between 110 and 220 volts, so it can be used overseas. Make sure that your computer is set up correctly.

If the terminal is running, but there is no login prompt, check the cables and brightness control.

What if you know the terminal is running but there's no login prompt? You hear the fan going, maybe you feel that the terminal is warm, but there's no sign of life. Lots of things might have gone wrong, but there are a few commonsense things you can try before you give up.

First, check the cables. The terminal may be powered on, but some other connections may have come loose.

Check that the keyboard is attached. If you have a mouse, make sure that it is attached as well. Nothing you do on your keyboard or with your mouse can be read by the computer unless the keyboard and mouse are attached to your terminal. If your keyboard or mouse was unattached, you may need to reboot the terminal before you can use it again.

If your terminal has a base that's separate from the monitor, make sure that the cable connecting them hasn't come loose. Also, the monitor may get its power through a separate power cord that connects to the computer or directly to the wall outlet.

On UNIX, it is unlikely that the machine you use is "stand-alone." Most likely, you use a terminal that must be connected to a network in order to run properly. So you need to pay extra-special attention to your network connector. The network connector may be a T-shaped adaptor attached to the back of your terminal, it might be something that looks like a phone cord, or it might be a small serial connector with anywhere from nine to 25 pins. Some machines may have a small LED indicator at the back that shows whether the network is active. The indicator will be either on the terminal itself or on a transceiver that's plugged into the terminal.

Embarrassment keeps you checking

One day I came in bright and early (7 AM) and I couldn't log in. My terminal didn't work. All I saw was a blank screen.

I pressed return several times and flicked the power switch. Since I wasn't a "computer person," I got some other work and sat down to wait.

An hour later, Peter came in. He was an MIT graduate. He could help! He turned the terminal off and on again, listened for the motor, and then found a small dial on the bottom of the monitor. The brightness control knob was turned all the way down.

After you're embarrassed once, you'll always remember to check.

Linda Lamb

Finally, check the brightness control knob. If this was accidentally turned all the way down, your screen will be dark and you won't be able to see the login prompt (or anything else).

If everything is plugged in and connected, reboot and try again.

Maybe you see nothing on the screen, or maybe all you see is gibberish. Many times, you can clear up the problem by simply rebooting the terminal. Following are some sample problems that can be resolved by rebooting:

- If the terminal normally boots over a network, there may have been a temporary problem with the network or with the host machine. Turn the terminal off and on again and see if it boots.

  A common time to have login problems is after a power outage, especially if your terminal needs the host computer in order to boot (as some X terminals do). During a power outage, both the terminal and the computer (server) lose power at the same time. When the power comes back on, however, the terminal resets itself faster than the computer. (The computer has to go through a much longer and more complex start-up procedure.) So if the terminal needs the host computer in order to boot, the reset will fail and your terminal will leave you with some indecipherable error messages.

  Rebooting the terminal when the host computer is up and running again will restore the terminal to a working state.

- If your screen shows gibberish, this could have several causes.

  ASCII terminals sometimes get into weird states because of special control sequences that are sent to them. For example, your terminal might display text in all caps, in reverse video, or in just plain gibberish—e.g., you might press the letter "a" and see "^]c4d." Or you might press the letter "a" and see a Greek alpha (α).

  A special control sequence could have been sent to your terminal when an arm brushed against the keyboard, or if you read a binary file. Try pressing the Break key or turn the terminal off and on. Rebooting resets the terminal to its default state.

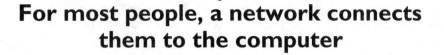

For most people, a network connects them to the computer

People often think that they have a computer at their desks, especially if they are used to working on PCs or Macintosh computers. On a UNIX system, it is less common for someone to have a complete computer system in their office. You still have a screen to read from and a keyboard to type on, but the files you look at or the programs that you run could live on a computer somewhere else.

UNIX machines are multi-user machines, which means that you may be sharing the machine with many other users. Obviously, if many people are sharing the same machine, they can't all have the physical computer at their desk.

Instead, most users have terminals, which connect to the main computer via a network. The main computer may be in the next room, on another floor in the building, or on the other side of the planet. Although you type your commands at your desk, your local terminal doesn't know what to do with the command. Instead, it just tells the computer over the network what keys you typed or where you moved your mouse; then, the computer tells the terminal what to display on the screen.

Think of the terminal as the translator for a visiting statesman at the United Nations: all the terminal does is convey the messages. It's the computer that makes the policy.

There are two types of terminals: character-based terminals (also known as ASCII terminals or dumb terminals) and X terminals (also known as X servers). A character-based terminal, such as a vt100, can only display a single window of text, usually limited to 24 lines and 80 columns of characters. An X terminal can display graphics and multiple windows. With both X terminals and character terminals, the terminal is useless without the main computer. When the main computer is not running, or when the network connection to the main computer is broken, you can't use the terminal.

Some users do have a dedicated UNIX machine on their desk, called a workstation. When logging in at a workstation, you may not need the network in order to log in, so it's possible that you will be able to log in successfully regardless of the network connection. However, many sites are set up so that even if you have a workstation, your login information, files, and applications still depend on a larger computer elsewhere on the network.

- If you have an X terminal and all you get is a blank screen, it may be that its login connection to your host needs to be restarted. This happens most often when your host computer has gone down. You can restart the login connection by turning the terminal off and on again. (There may also be a gentler way of reconnecting to the host computer, depending on what sort of X terminal you use.)

If you still can't get the terminal to respond, let your system administrator know.

Before you report your own problem to a system administrator, check other terminals like yours to see if they are also having problems. It's possible that the host computer went down and no one can log in. It's also possible that something went wrong with the network software, with your gateway to the rest of the network, or that the physical network was a casualty of the construction on the fourth floor of your office building.

None of these are things you can do anything about, but at least it identifies the problem as the administrator's and not yours. Make sure that someone's notified the administrator that something's gone wrong, and then be patient until it's fixed.

When you tell your administrator about your problem, be sure to tell her what kind of equipment you have, and what solutions you have already tried. For example, if you can't log in at a character-based terminal, then the administrator would go through a different series of steps than she would for an X terminal. Your administrator may also know about special issues for particular terminal models. For example, she may know that the Num Lock key on some terminals prevents mouse clicks from registering, etc.

The computer checks your login name and password.

Once you have a login prompt, you can type in your login name and your password. The computer lets you log in under that name only if you give the correct password for that login account.

The login name you have been assigned on your system might follow any number of naming conventions. At some sites, you can request a specific login name (if no one else already uses it). At other sites, you're stuck with what they give you. It might be your first name. It might be your last name. It might be your initials. It might be your first name with your last initial, your first initial with your last name, or it might be your nickname. Some larger sites have other conventions, such as your initials with a three-digit number after it.

Your password is initially set by your system administrator. When you first get your account, your system administrator should tell you your login name and password. (The administrator will also ask you to change your password as soon as possible.)

If you don't know your login name or password, you'll have to ask your system administrator.

Remember that UNIX is *case-sensitive*, meaning that lowercase letters are considered distinct from their uppercase counterparts. If your login name is *lois*, then you have to type *lois* when logging in, not *Lois* or *LOIS*. Make sure that you type your login name and password exactly as it was given to you.

If your login isn't accepted, it's most likely a typing error. Try again.

What if you try to log in, but your login isn't accepted?

Of course, the first thing to do is to try again, slowly—since you might have mistyped your password. It's easy to mistype a password, since you can't see it as you type it. Also, remember that truism of keyboard operators everywhere, that as soon as anyone's watching over your shoulder you can't spell your own name. Before you decide that something's actually wrong, calm down and try again.

What do you do when you can't log in?

When I have trouble logging in, I first look to see if it's anything that I've done. Then I double-check hardware. And then I wander out to see if other people are having the problem. If those checks fail, I ask for help.

Joan Callahan

If you still can't log in, try another terminal to rule out equipment problems.

Once you've determined that you've typed your login name and password correctly, but you still can't log in, here are some other things to try:

- Try logging in at another person's terminal. This way, you make sure to discount problems with your keyboard or terminal. If you can log in somewhere else, it's possible that you just need to reboot your terminal and you'll be fine again (especially for X terminals).
- See if anyone else is having this problem. This way you can find out if something is wrong with just your account, or whether something's wrong with the systemwide password database.

Passwords are stored in a database.

To verify that your login name and password are correct, the computer searches for your login name in a password database. This database is kept either in a file called */etc/passwd* on your system, or in a systemwide database maintained elsewhere on your network.

Today, many modern UNIX systems don't use */etc/passwd*. Instead, they use something called Network Information Services (NIS), also known as Yellow Pages. The idea behind NIS is that it helps you maintain the same login names and passwords across several different machines. If you have more than one UNIX system on the same network, then it's likely that you want a login account on all of the machines. In addition, you want to make sure that if you change your password on one machine, it is changed on all other machines as well.

To see your entry in the database, first try running *ypmatch name passwd.* For example:

```
% ypmatch lois passwd
lois:ctA433xqXp/Q:183:100:Lois Lane:/home/lois:/bin/csh
```

If you get the message "Command not found," "no such map in server's domain," or "ypbind is not running on this machine," then use the *grep* command to search for your name in */etc/passwd*:

```
% grep lois /etc/passwd
lois:ctA433xqXp/Q:183:100:Lois Lane:/home/lois:/bin/csh
```

The fields in a *passwd* entry are separated by colons. There are usually seven fields in all. The user's login name is shown in the first field, followed by a colon. The next field shows her password, in an encrypted format. It is encrypted so that, although everyone can see the *passwd* entry, you can't learn anyone's actual password from it.

On some systems, you might just see an "x" in the password field, while the actual encrypted passwords reside in another file.

The rest of the *passwd* entry isn't important right now. However, you might be interested in the comment field, which usually contains the user's full name. If you don't know someone's login name, searching *passwd* entries for that person's full name is one way to find it. (Chapter 7 discusses another method, using the *finger* command.)

Login accounts may be disabled by the system administrator.

Computer accounts are occasionally disabled on a system. With his account disabled, the user still has an entry in the *passwd* file, but he cannot log in.

There are several reasons why a login account may be disabled:

- Some companies have a policy of disabling accounts as soon as an employee stops working there. A university may disable an account as soon as a student graduates. The main reason to do this is for security. It's the same reason you ask ex-roommates to leave their keys behind when they move out.

- Other, friendlier, companies don't remove accounts when people quit, but they may disable a password if that person hasn't logged in for a while (for example, if they haven't used the account for a year).

- Some system administrators disable accounts that have passwords that are easily guessed, such as words in the dictionary or names that are the same as the login name.

Choose a password that not even your friends can guess

A friend of mine in college once forgot her password. I sat down with her, remembered the name of some guy she had a fling with over winter break, and typed it in for her.

Sure enough, it worked. I looked at her smugly, and then I saw that her face had turned beet red. It was truly embarrassing to her that she had been so obsessed about this guy to use his name as her password, and that now I knew it too. To this day I wish I hadn't tried to be so smart and embarrassed her like that.

Tanya Herlick
administrator

Once upon a time, our company didn't have passwords, not even for the superuser. We weren't on the Internet or any other network connecting to other companies, so we didn't see the need. We all worked in one office and anyone could log in as anyone else at will. We were naive, but happy.

One evening, someone logged in as root over the modem, and we never knew who it was. We disconnected the modem before he or she could do any damage, and gave everyone passwords. We still resisted enforcing real security, however, so we initially gave everyone the same password, "friend."

Today, we're on the Internet, we all have different passwords, and we enforce rules on making sure that they are changed frequently and that they're hard to break. But sometimes I think wistfully back to when we thought everyone could be trusted. By connecting to the Internet, I feel as if we moved to a big, faceless city from a small,

friendly town.

Linda Walsh

They find these accounts by running special "cracking" software, which deliberately tries to guess passwords in order to pinpoint the ones that are easy targets.

- Some companies ask users to change their passwords frequently (for example, every six months) and disable the accounts of users who don't respond to the warnings.

- Even the most tolerant companies will disable accounts of users who abuse their privileges.

You can ask another user to check if your account was disabled in the password database.

If you can't log in, it's possible that your account was disabled. If you can find someone else who's logged in, have them check your entry in the password database.

There are three ways that you can tell if an account has been disabled:

- If you see an asterisk in the password field (the second field), then no one can log in under that account.

  ```
  lois:*:189:100:Lois Lane:/home/lois:/bin/csh
  ```

- If you see something like *nosh* or *noshell* or *none* in the last field, then the password will be accepted, but the person will not be able to access her account.

  ```
  lois:4y19O/wqZ0s:189:100:Lois Lane:/home/lois:/bin/noshell
  ```

- The *passwd* entry might have been removed completely (although this isn't likely, since administrators don't like to reuse login names or user IDs).

If you've forgotten your password, you'll need to ask your system administrator for help.

Forgetting passwords happens most often on a new account or on an account you don't use very often.

If this happens to you...sorry, our bag of tricks is empty. There isn't anything else you can do except ask your administrator to assign you a new password (which you'll be expected to change as soon as possible).

(Your administrator can't just tell you what your password was. Passwords are encrypted, so they are impossible to recover.)

When you're assigned a new password, log in with it, and then change your password to one that only you know. Change your password with the *passwd* command. The *passwd* command first prompts you for your old password and then asks you for the new one. It asks you for the new password twice, to make sure that you haven't made a typo. For example:

```
% passwd
Changing NIS password for lmui on ruby.
Old password: [type current password]
New password: [type new password]
Retype new password: [repeat new password]
NIS entry changed on ruby
```

The *passwd* command doesn't show the password as you type it, so that people looking over your shoulder won't see it.

Here's a bit of computer etiquette: respect the passwords of your friends and coworkers. Don't try to look over people's shoulders when they type their passwords, and don't be shy about asking them to look away while you type your own.

Don't depend on written reminders

One day, a coworker arrived from our California office and couldn't log in. It turned out that her password was taken from a newspaper article that was posted in her office, and since she didn't have it with her, she couldn't remember her password!

Her password consisted of the first letters of each word in the article's headline. So she had to call the California office and ask someone to read her the headline until she could reconstruct her password.

Tanya Herlick
administrator

Your password gives someone else a lot of power

Your password is the only thing preventing other users from logging in as you, with all your privileges. If someone breaks into your computer account, she can:

- Read all your personal files
- Remove all your files
- Look at other sensitive files that you have access to on the system
- Insult your boss in email, under your name
- Post an obnoxious message to every newsgroup on the Internet, under your name
- Sabotage the system by planting destructive programs, such as worms or trojan horses

Letting someone log into your machine makes it easy for them to probe the system for security holes, in much the same way a robber would "case" a convenience store. If they don't know what type of safe there is or where it is located, it makes the store that much harder to rob.

If it takes a few extra minutes to think up a good password, it's time well spent. A bad password can ruin your day (your career, even).

People try to crack passwords with programs or with personal knowledge

Someone who is interested in breaking into your account can run a program designed specifically for cracking passwords. These programs can be run automatically. So someone could just let a cracking program run overnight, trying thousands of passwords on your account.

The sorts of passwords that are easily "cracked" are:

- Words in the dictionary
- Letters that appear in sequence on the keyboard such as "qwerty" or "qazxsw"
- Any sequence of numbers

- Proper names (especially your own)

Evil strangers aren't the only people who might want to break into your account. Well-meaning (or not so well-meaning) coworkers might also try to break in—possibly just to play a friendly prank, possibly to get you fired. Just because people have good intentions doesn't mean that they have good judgment as well.

So avoid passwords that people who know you might guess. Don't use your address, license plate number, phone number, pet's name, birthday, or the name of your favorite cousin. Don't use any portion or combination of these, either. Don't combine one of these with some letters capitalized, or with a trailing "1", or anything like that.

Also, avoid things that have to do with your hobbies or interests. If you're a die-hard Pittsburgh Pirates fan, the password "21-Clemente" would be easily guessed by someone who knew you. If you play bridge, "1NoTrump" is one of the first things I would try.

Choosing a good password

How do you choose a "good" password? A password is like a locked door. You want one that is hard to break into. With a password, you are looking for a string of characters that are difficult to guess, either by a human or by a computer program. In general, good passwords:

- Have both uppercase and lowercase letters
- Have digits and/or punctuation as well as letters
- Are easy to remember so that they do not have to be written down
- Are seven or eight characters long
- Can be typed quickly so that someone cannot follow what you type by looking over your shoulder

What you need to know about logging in

How do you come up with a password that you can actually remember? Some suggestions for picking a good password:

- Take two short words and combine them with a special character or number, like robot4any or eye-con.

- Put together an acronym that's special to you, like Notfsw (None of this fancy stuff works).

If you must write it down

Users are often admonished to "never write down a password." A password that you memorize is more secure than a password that you write down. If you must write down your password in order to remember it, follow these commonsense precautions:

- Do not identify your password as a password.

- Do not include the name of the account or the phone number of the computer on the same piece of paper.

- Do not attach the password to your terminal, keyboard, any part of your computer, or to a bulletin board or in a top desk drawer.

- Mix in some "noise" characters or scramble the written version of the password in a way that you will remember, that makes the written version different from the real password. For example, if your password were robot4any, you could write down robot2any or Robot4Any, etc.

- Never record a password online and never send a password by electronic mail.

In addition, beware of embedding your password in another application. For example, users who sometimes log in from a PC or Macintosh might try to save time with a script that supplies both the user name and password. But this means that anyone else who turns on that PC has access to their UNIX account.

Password hints are adapted from the O'Reilly & Associates Inc. book *Practical UNIX Security*, by Simson Garfinkel and Gene Spafford. (That book is aimed at system administrators.)

If you can't log in under X, then something may be wrong with the .xsession file

If you use an X terminal, then you might find that your password is accepted, but you still can't log in. If this happens, you may have a problem with a file called *.xsession* in your home directory. The *.xsession* file specifies commands that are run when you log in under X.

You can bypass any .xsession problems by typing CTRL-Return after your password

Luckily, there is an escape route you can try. By pressing CTRL-Return instead of Return after typing in your password, your *.xsession* file is ignored. Instead, you get a single xterm window.

If you can log in using CTRL-Return, you know for sure that the problem is with your *.xsession* file. You can use this xterm window to edit or change permissions on your *.xsession* file, so that you will be able to log in properly next time.

.xsession must be an executable file

One reason you can't log in may be that your *.xsession* script isn't executable.

An executable file is one that can be run as a command. One way to tell if a file is executable is by listing it with the *ls –F* command; if it appears with an asterisk (*) after the filename, then it's executable. Try running *ls –F .xsession* as soon as you can:

```
% ls -F .xsession
.xsession
```

Here (as shown above), *.xsession* is not executable, and you need to use the *chmod +x* command on it. (See Chapter 4 for more information on executable files and changing file permissions.)

```
% chmod +x .xsession
% ls -F .xsession
.xsession*
```

After running chmod +x, the .xsession file appears with a trailing asterisk, so it is executable. Try to log in again now.

All but the last command in .xsession need to be run in the background

The *.xsession* file usually consists of a set of commands, just as you would type them on the command line. For example, here is a very simple *.xsession* file:

```
xterm &
xterm &
xclock &
xcalc &
twm
```

Here, we start two xterm windows, an xclock window, a calculator (xcalc), and a special program (called a window manager) called *twm*. The thing to notice is that all but the last line end in an ampersand (&). This is not arbitrary; it is necessary in order for your X login to function properly.

The commands with ampersands at the end are being run in the *background*, and the last command (*twm*) is being run in the *foreground*. Typical commands to run in the foreground are an xterm window or a window manager such as *twm, mwm, olwm,* or *fvwm.* When you exit your foreground program, you are logged out of X.

Quick Reference

of login troubleshooting

Information to find and keep

What is the best way to reboot my terminal?_____

_____

Are there any terminal peculiarities? _____

_____

For X users: what's the best way to get a new login

box? _____

_____

Terminal is dead. No hum. No lights.

Check the power supply. Is the power cord plugged
into both the electrical outlet and the computer? Is the
computer turned on? Is the outlet working? (Check
with an appliance such as a lamp.)

Terminal is running but not lit up

1. Check the cables and connectors; e.g., is the base
   connected to the monitor? Is the network connection plugged in?

2. If the monitor has a separate power cord, is that
   plugged in to a power outlet?

3. Check the brightness control knob.

4. Try rebooting.

Terminal shows gibberish

① Try rebooting. ② *break key before reboot.*

Can't type characters in the login box

Check that the keyboard and mouse are connected to
the terminal. Are there any lights on the keyboard that
aren't usually there, such as a Num Lock key or a
Program key that might prevent typing or mouse clicks?

Your login is not accepted

1. Type it over. Take your time.

2. Try logging in at another terminal, to see if the
   problem might be with your terminal.

3. Ask if others are having the same problem.

4. Ask for help from the system administrator.

Choosing a new password

1. Type the *passwd* command

   % passwd

2. Select a password of seven or eight characters, with
   uppercase and lowercase letters, digits, and punctuation, that is easy to remember without writing it
   down.

3. Type your new password. Repeat it when prompted.

On an X terminal, your password is accepted but you can't stay logged in

1. Try logging in again, but instead of typing Return
   after your password, type CTRL-Return.

2. Check that the *.xsession* file in your home directory
   is executable; type:

   % ls -F .xsession

   If the file is executable, there will be an asterisk
   after the filename. If not, make it executable:

   % chmod +x .xsession

   and try logging in again.

3. Check that the program listed in the last line of
   your *.xsession* file has no ampersand (&) at the end
   of the line. If the last line is ended with an ampersand, delete the ampersand and log in again.

CHAPTER 3

What you need to know about running programs

You run programs in UNIX by typing them on the command line.

On a UNIX system, you run programs by typing the name of the program on the command line and pressing Return. Usually, this is all you need to know.

However, sometimes a program may not work correctly. Or it may not work at all. Maybe you're not even sure what program you want to run.

Before you take your problem to the system administrator, you should learn something about how programs are run in UNIX. This chapter covers:

- What to do when you can't seem to run a command ("Command not found.")

- Why a program may not work properly

- How to find out more about a program's options and use

Users on X terminals or workstations may start programs via their graphical user interface, by selecting them from a menu, or by clicking a button. Many of the issues listed in this chapter can also apply to running programs from a GUI environment, but they may be a bit more complicated to fix. See your system administrator for information on how to properly configure your graphical user environment.

Knowing about commands

I don't know a lot of commands. I only use ones I've been shown. I sometimes wonder what commands or options would be useful to me that I don't even know exist.

Carol Vogt

The error "Command not found" means that the command isn't in your search path.

When you get the error "Command not found," it means that the computer searched everywhere it knew to look and couldn't find a program by that name.

You can control where the computer looks for commands, however. So "Command not found" doesn't necessarily mean that the program isn't anywhere on the system. It may just mean that you didn't give the computer enough information to find it. Before you ask your administrator for help, there are a few things you can do:

- Check the name of the command and confirm that you didn't make a typo on the command line.

- Make sure that the command is installed on the system.

- If the command is installed on your system, make sure the computer knows where to look.

Check if the command was misspelled.

Misspelling a command is one of the most common mistakes people can make. Check for the following:

- Spaces between the command name and options. (If you don't include spaces, the command thinks the option is part of the name of the command.)

- Characters that you may be reading incorrectly—for example, is that number 1 really a letter l?

- Case sensitivity. Remember that UNIX is case-sensitive. You can't exchange a lowercase letter with an uppercase letter or vice versa and still expect it to work.

- Words that may need to be substituted. Is "filename" supposed to be replaced with the name of an actual file? Is "n" supposed to be replaced by a number?

What you need to know about running programs

Most programs reside in bin directories.

Each UNIX system has literally hundreds of programs installed on it. Some programs are distributed with the operating system, and others are bought from third-party vendors. In addition, some programs (such as Emacs) are distributed "free," and some may have been developed exclusively for your site.

Each program is stored like any other file on the UNIX system. The difference is that programs are *executable files*, meaning that they have special permission to be run as a command. Other than being executable, programs are just files like any other file installed on the system. (This doesn't mean that you can read or edit all of them, since many executable files are stored in a nonreadable format called *binary format*. But you can list and copy them as you can other files.)

Programs are usually installed in a directory called *bin*—for example, in */bin*, */usr/bin*, */usr/local/bin*, etc. When you type *ls*, you are really running the program */bin/ls*. When you type *grep*, you are really running */usr/bin/grep*.

You can run a program using its full pathname.

One way to run a program is to execute it using its full pathname. For example, I know that the *date* program is installed on my system as */bin/date*. I can run the program by typing */bin/date* directly on the command line:

```
% /bin/date
Tue Nov  8 16:41:51 EST 1994
```

This is the same thing I would get if I just typed *date*. When you type *date* on the command line, you are essentially using a shortcut for typing */bin/date*.

You can run a program without its full pathname because of your command "search path."

So how do you get from typing */bin/date* on the command line to only typing *date*?

"Command not found."

I used to work at a small company that distributed its own version of UNIX. One day I took a tech support call from some guy who complained that none of the commands worked. The most basic commands weren't being recognized, including pwd and ls. All the user got was the error "Command not found."

I had no idea what to do. Normally I would ask the user to check his search path, but the user couldn't even do that. Finally, I asked him to cd to the /bin directory and learned that even cd complained "Command not found."

What's wrong with this? cd is a "built-in" command. It doesn't need to be in the search path.

It turned out that the user was typing all the commands with the Caps Lock key pressed. He was a PC user who didn't understand that UNIX is case-sensitive.

Paul Kleppner

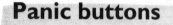

Panic buttons

It's happened to all of us. You run a command and then scream, "What have I done?!?"

Sometimes it's too late. For example, if I accidentally ran the *rm* command when I intended to type *mv...*, as soon as I pressed Return, it was too late.

But often there is a way to stop a command.

Interrupt commands or mail messages with CTRL-C

When a command is still running in the foreground on the command line, you can usually stop the command by pressing CTRL-C. You know a command is still running in the foreground if you haven't gotten your command-line prompt back yet. When you type CTRL-C, it appears on the screen as ^C.

You might want to interrupt a command because it is dangerous, or just because you don't want to wait for it to complete. For example:

```
% who
^C
%
```

You can also use CTRL-C when composing messages in most character-based mailers. By typing CTRL-C twice, you can discard a message instead of sending it.

Cancel print jobs with lprm

If you send a job to a printer and then want to cancel it, you can use the *lprm* command to remove print jobs. To cancel just one print job, use *lprm* with the job number (which you can learn via the *lpq* command). For example:

```
% lpq
...
2nd lois 422 standard input 38403 bytes
% lprm 422
```

If you know that you only have one job on the printer queue, you can also just use *lprm* without the printer job. This removes all your print jobs.

```
% lprm
```

lprm is most useful when you send a big job to the printer and then saunter over and see that something on page 1 was wrong, and the entire job needs to be resent. Or when you send a small job to a printer and discover that you're stuck behind a 200-page document. Before reprinting the entire job, you can stop the current job with *lprm* and help save a tree by eliminating all that wasted paper.

Individual programs may also have ways of being interrupted

Many programs have their own "escape hatches."

- The *telnet* program usually lets you escape from a connection to a site by typing CTRL-] and then *quit*.

- Popular World Wide Web browsers let you cancel the current transmission by clicking on an icon, e.g. a spinning world icon at the upper-right corner of the window or a "stop" button. (This comes in useful when you realize that a 9MB audio snippet of Gregorian chants is being transferred to your local system.)

HP-UX
npdel > delete job
npcancel > delete entire queue

When you type the word *date* on the command line, the computer looks through the system for a command by that name. It doesn't look everywhere. Instead, the computer searches for the command only in those directories listed in your *search path*. If your search path contains the directories */usr/bin*, */usr/ucb*, */bin*, and */usr/local/bin*, the computer first looks for */usr/bin/date*. If it doesn't find the *date* program in */usr/bin*, then it looks for */usr/ucb/date*. And so on, until it finds */bin/date*.

Once UNIX finds a program by the name *date* in a directory in your search path, it executes that program.

You can find the directory where a program is installed with the whereis or which command.

If you want to know a program's full pathname, you can use the *whereis* program. The *whereis* program looks in a predefined set of directories for the named program.

```
% whereis who
who: /usr/bin/who /usr/man/man1/who.1
```

This tells you that the *who* program is in */usr/bin*. (*whereis* also tells you where you can find online documentation for the program.)

Although *whereis* doesn't tell you about *all* programs installed on your system, it's an excellent place to start.

One problem with *whereis* is that since it looks in a built-in directory path, it may not find programs that are not installed in a "standard" directory. At our office we have many programs installed into */usr/local/txtools/bin*, but *whereis* doesn't know about them. For example, the *rcsgrep* command is installed in that directory:

```
% ls -F /usr/local/txtools/bin/rcsgrep
/usr/local/txtools/bin/rcsgrep*
```

But *whereis* can't find it, because it isn't in any of the "standard" directories that *whereis* usually examines:

```
% whereis rcsgrep
rcsgrep:
```

A user who can't run *rcsgrep,* therefore, has no way to find out where it is installed using *whereis.* Without knowing where a

Unlike PCs and Macs, UNIX treats all files the same

A big difference between UNIX and Mac/PC environments is file typing. DOS and Windows try to make assumptions of what a file is based on its extension, like .bin or .txt. Macs store information about the program that created the file along with the file.

UNIX just treats everything the same—files, binaries, executables, you name it. Using a PC or Mac mentality, every UNIX command is an "App" or "utility."

A lot of people here call text files "vi files" or "Emacs files" because that's what they use to create it. They're used to an application "owning" the file, like you'd say "a WordPerfect file" or "an Excel file." They are amazed when they find out they can use that file in email or open it in another editor.

Eric Pearce
administrator

command is installed, you can't know what directory to add to your search path.

One possibility is to find another user who can run *rcsgrep* to use the *which* program on it. Like *whereis*, *which* tells you the full pathname of a program—but *which* uses your search path, not just a "standard" directory path. Of course, you can't use *which* yourself to find a program that isn't in your own search path. But if you can find other users who *can* run the *rcsgrep* program, they can use *which* to tell you where the program is installed.

```
% which rcsgrep
/usr/local/txtools/bin/rcsgrep
```

This tells me that the *rcsgrep* program is in */usr/local/txtools/ bin*. If I add this directory to my search path, I will be able to run the *rcsgrep* program the next time I log in.

Add directories to your search path.

If you find out that the program you want to run is in a directory that isn't in your command search path, you can add that directory to your search path.

For example, suppose you want to run the *vn* program, but you get "Command not found":

```
% vn
vn: Command not found.
```

Using *whereis*, you might learn that *vn* is installed in */usr/local/bin*:

```
% whereis vn
vn: /usr/local/bin/vn
```

You can always run the *vn* program using its full pathname of */usr/local/bin/vn*. But if you want to run it just by typing *vn*, then you have to add the directory to your search path.

The way you do this depends on how you are configured. What you need to do is look for a file in your home directory called *.cshrc*, *.profile*, *.bashrc*, *.tcshrc*, etc.

In the file, you should see a line containing a list of directories. For example, in a *.cshrc* or *.tcshrc* file, you may see a line resembling:

```
set path=(/bin /usr/bin /usr/bin/X11)
```

In *.profile* or *.bashrc*, you might see a line like this:

```
PATH=/bin:/usr/bin:/usr/bin/X11
```

In one case, the directories are separated by spaces and placed within parentheses. In the other, directories are separated by colons.

To add a new directory, just put it at the end of the list. For example, to add */usr/local/bin*, you would change the above lines to read either:

```
PATH=/bin:/usr/bin:/usr/bin/X11:/usr/local/bin
```

or:

```
set path=(/bin /usr/bin /usr/bin/X11 /usr/local/bin)
```

The next time you log in after editing your startup file, you will be able to run the *vn* command, as well as any other command that is installed in */usr/local/bin*.

The only thing to be careful of in adding new directories is that you don't accidentally insert a carriage return (which is easy to do if you use an editor like *vi* that automatically wraps lines). If you do want to include a carriage return within your search path, precede the carriage return with a backslash (\).

The command might run, but not work correctly.

Sometimes the command seems to run, but it doesn't work as advertised. Any number of things might have happened:

- There may be more than one version of the command online, and you may be running the wrong version.
- You may have an *alias* set up for the command.
- Your environment may not be set up correctly.
- You might not be using the command correctly.
- You may not have permission to run the command.
- Your computer is out to get you. (Just kidding.)

There are plenty of reasons why a program may not work correctly, and we can't tell you about all of them. But here are some things that you might need to know about when things go awry.

Knowing about commands

On a Macintosh, it's easy to find out what you can do. You pull down menus and go through the options.

But with UNIX, nothing's that simple. You have to know things before you can do anything.

Allen Noren

There may be more than one version of the same command on your system.

If there is more than one version of a program online, *whereis* tells you about all the versions that it finds. For example, on our system we have two versions of *ls*:

```
% whereis ls
ls: /usr/5bin/ls /usr/bin/ls
```

The reason there are two versions of the same command has to do with the evolution of UNIX. The *ls* command developed differently on different versions of UNIX. Today, some modern operating systems provide both versions, so users can choose the one they're used to. On our system, the System V versions of programs are stored in */usr/5bin*.

When there are two versions of a program, the one executed is the one earliest in your search path.

On our system, there are two versions of the *ls* command: */usr/bin/ls* and */usr/5bin/ls*. The one that is executed when a user types *ls* depends on the order that */usr/5bin* and */usr/bin* are listed in the user's search path.

For example, if a search path reads:

```
/bin:/usr/bin:/usr/ucb:/usr/5bin:/usr/local/bin
```

Then the version of *ls* that is installed in */usr/bin* is the one that is encountered first and is therefore the one that is executed. If you wanted to use the other version of *ls*, one way to do it is to edit your search path to put */usr/5bin* earlier in your path:

```
/bin:/usr/5bin:/usr/bin:/usr/ucb:/usr/local/bin
```

Beware, however, that this means you also get other *5bin* versions of commands, which you may not want. A better way of using your preferred *ls* is to define an alias.

You can have "aliases" for commands.

Most users have the ability to define *aliases* for commands. An alias is another way to "shorthand" a command. For example, if you often *cd* to the */usr/local/txtools/font/ps* directory, and you don't want to type out the complete command all the time, you

What you need to know about running programs

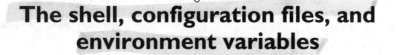

The shell, configuration files, and environment variables

The program that gives you your UNIX prompt and processes the commands you type there is called a shell. There are many different shells that run on UNIX systems, but the two basic families are the Bourne shell and the C shell. The shell is technically just another program on the system— for example, the Korn shell is */bin/ksh*, and the C shell is */bin/csh*.

When you are given a login account, you are also assigned a shell. The shell you are given determines what commands you can run, what features you can use with the commands (such as aliasing, file-name completion, or command-line editing), and the name of your account's startup file.

Shell Startup Files

Once you log in, the shell reads a startup file in your home directory to set things like your search path and your command-line prompt. Korn shell (*ksh*) users are configured by the *.profile* file and C shell (*csh*) users are configured by the *.cshrc* and *.login* file. If you don't see these files in your home directory when you type *ls*, try running *ls –a* instead:

```
% ls -a
.cshrc .login Mail personal
```

If you edit your shell startup file, be sure to make a copy of it first. For example:

```
% cp .cshrc .cshrc.old
```

That way, you can go back to the older, saved file if you make an editing mistake. A mistake in this file won't prevent you from logging in, but it can make your environment very difficult to work in.

Environment Variables

Your shell startup file defines your search path and sets environment variables for you. Environment variables are special values that are passed to other programs. For example, if you define the PRINTER environment variable, setting it to the name of a printer, then all your print jobs will go to that printer (unless you explicitly direct them to another printer), whether you start your print job from the command line or from within an application.

The syntax you use to set environment variables depends on what shell you use. If you use *csh* or *tcsh*, use the setenv command in your *.cshrc* or *.tcshrc* file:

```
setenv PRINTER ibis
```

In *sh*, *ksh*, or *bash*, you have to set the variable and then "export" it in *.profile* or *.bashrc*:

```
PRINTER=ibis
export PRINTER
```

Or as a shortcut in *ksh* or *bash*:

```
export PRINTER=ibis
```

In addition to the environment variables you set in your shell startup file, there are also some that are automatically set when you log in. To list the values of all your environment variables, type:

```
% printenv
```

To see the value of a single environment variable, supply it as an argument to *printenv*:

```
% printenv PRINTER
ibis
```

Your search path itself is kept in an environment variable called PATH. Other important environment variables are TERM and MANPATH.

can make an alias for it. If you always want to run a command with certain options—for example, if you always want to see slashes after directory names when you type *ls*—then you can alias the *ls* command to "ls –F".

The way you define an alias depends on what shell you use. If you use the C shell or *tcsh*, then in your *.cshrc* or *.tcshrc* you might enter lines like these:

```
alias cdfont 'cd /usr/local/txtools/font/ps'
alias lf 'ls -F'
```

If you use the Korn shell or *bash*:

```
alias cdfont='cd /usr/local/txtools/font/ps'
alias lf='ls -F'
```

If there are two versions of a command on your system, you can use aliases to make sure you run the version you prefer. In many ways, this is preferable to changing your search path to ensure that you get the version of *ls* that you want.

```
alias ls '/usr/5bin/ls'
```

Sometimes you can get in trouble with aliases. For example, if you want to always *ls* a directory after you *cd* to it, you might be tempted to define the following alias:

```
alias cdls 'cd; ls'
```

However, this means that every time you run *cdls*, you'll *cd* to your home directory. In the C shell or *tcsh*, you can use the special "\!*" syntax to pass the rest of the command line to *cd*:

```
alias cdls 'cd \!*; ls'
```

Now when you say "cdls /usr/local," what the computer runs is "cd /usr/local; ls," which is what you want.

To see a list of all the aliases you have defined, use the *alias* command without any arguments:

```
% alias
lf      ls -F
cdls    cd; ls
cdfont  cd /usr/local/txtools/font/ps
```

The which command tells you what version of a program you are using or whether you have an alias.

The *which* program tells you what version of a program comes first in your search path. For example:

```
% which ls
/usr/bin/ls
```

This tells me that I'm using the version of *ls* that is installed in */usr/bin*.

If you have an alias defined, *which* reports the alias instead, so you can use it as a general all-purpose tool to learn what's going on. For example:

```
% which ls
ls: aliased to ls -aCF
```

If a program isn't working properly, you could be running a different version of it.

When programs don't work the way they're supposed to, one thing to investigate is that you're running the correct version of the program.

For example, when I run *ls* to list files, I'm used to seeing the files ordered in multiple columns. So I was surprised one day when I saw that all my files were being listed in a single column, but none of the filenames were long enough to require a single-column listing:

```
% ls
Mail
discards
discards.backup
finger.mail
mysteries
notes.lmui
schedule
```

What was happening was that I recently changed my search path so */usr/5bin* appeared before */usr/bin*. Using the *which* command, I learned that the version of *ls* I was running was */usr/5bin/ls*.

Knowing about commands

The hardest part of UNIX is knowing how to find information— the apropos command only goes so far.

Ellen Siever

```
% which ls
/usr/5bin/ls
```

What I'm used to is */usr/bin/ls*.

```
% /usr/bin/ls
Mail         discards.backup  mysteries        schedule
discards     finger.mail      notes
```

There might also be permission problems.

Finally, you might have to worry about permissions when a program doesn't work correctly. For a program to work properly, the following permissions need to be granted:

- You need execute permission for the program itself.
- You need read permission for all files that the program opens for reading (although some programs are installed with special permissions to circumvent this.)
- You need write permission for all files that the program needs to change.

When you have a permissions problem running a program, you'll get an error like "Permission denied," or you might see the name of a file followed by "cannot open." What you need to do is learn what files or commands you need permission for and then have permission extended to you. If it isn't obvious from the error message what kind of permission you need, try using the *man* command. On many manpages, there is a FILES section near the end that lists some of the files that the command needs to use.

Chapter 4 covers permissions in more detail.

The TERM environment variable tells programs what type of terminal you use.

Some programs need to know what sort of terminal you have.

Character-based terminals and terminal emulators are all different. Each uses different sequences of characters (called *escape sequences*) for different purposes. For example, when you press the F1 key on a Digital vt100 terminal, it generates a different set of characters than if you press F1 on a Wyse–75 terminal. Each terminal also recognizes special commands to tell it where to place characters, where to place the cursor, whether to clear the screen, etc.—and each terminal uses different commands.

Simple programs, like *ls* or *who*, don't do anything fancy, so they don't need to know about differences between terminals. But programs that have to do anything more complicated need to first know what sort of terminal you use. For example, an editor like *vi* or Emacs needs to know how to position a line at the top and bottom of your screen, how to move the cursor up, down, left, and right, etc.

The TERM environment variable is defined to tell programs about your terminal. TERM just has the name of a terminal type, such as vt100 or wyse–75. When programs start up, they look for the value of TERM to know what sort of escape sequences it uses.

If TERM is not set, programs may not run.

If your TERM environment variable is not defined, then programs have no way to know how to move the cursor or output text at the top of a screen. If you try running Emacs without TERM defined, you'll see something like this:

```
% emacs
Please set the environment variable TERM; see tset(1).
```

Emacs won't run at all without TERM defined.

vi, on the other hand, will run, but you sort of wish it hadn't.

```
% vi
Visual needs addressable cursor or upline capability
:
```

vi cannot run without knowing how to move the cursor. So its response is to put you in its underlying editor, *ex*. Most people don't know *ex*, or don't know that they know it; *vi* users may recognize it as the "colon prompt" at the bottom of a *vi* window and realize that they can exit by typing q and Return.

You may be prompted for your terminal type at login time

Your login account may be set up so that after logging in, you see a prompt saying something like the following:

TERM=(vt100)

This message comes from the *tset* command, which sets your terminal type for you. It gives you an opportunity to specify a different terminal type.

In this example, if you press Return, then your terminal type is set to vt100. However, you can also type in the name of another terminal type and then press Return.

The TERM=(vt100) prompt confuses many new users. But the rule of thumb is, unless you know what you're doing, just press Return. If it's wrong, you'll know soon enough.

If TERM is set wrong, you may get gibberish.

If the TERM environment variable is set incorrectly, you may get an error message complaining about a nonexistent terminal type. For example:

```
% setenv TERM wyse-747
% vi
wyse-747: Unknown terminal type
Visual needs addressable cursor or upline capability
:q
```

However, it's more likely that you have used a legitimate terminal type, but one that's wrong for this terminal. If so, the program will run merrily along, but the terminal will look as if it is possessed. Characters will be garbled. Your cursor may be placed at an odd position.

The thing to do is to remember that the garbled text only affects what you see: the program itself is working fine and should properly interpret what you type. So quit out as you normally would (CTRL-X CTRL-C in Emacs, :q in *vi*) and then find out what the correct terminal type is from your system administrator (or someone else who knows).

Use the man command to learn how to use a command.

Knowing what command to run isn't always enough. You might also need to know how to run the command. For that, use the *man* command, which tells you what the command does and what command-line options there are for it.

```
% man wc

WC(1)  USER COMMANDS                        WC(1)

NAME
     wc - count lines, words and characters

SYNOPSIS
     wc [ -lwc ] [ filename ... ]
```

DESCRIPTION

```
    wc counts lines, words, and characters in filenames, or in
    the standard input if no filename appears.  It also keeps
    a total count for all named files.  A word is a string of
    characters delimited by SPACE, TAB, or NEWLINE characters.
```

This documentation is usually distributed with the program. It is called a manual page or, more affectionately, a *manpage* (rhymes with rampage, sort of).

Try the apropos command (or man -k) to find the name of a command.

If you know what you want to do, but you don't know what command does it, another thing to try is the *apropos* command. *apropos* prints out a one-line summary of commands, based on a keyword search.

For example, suppose you want to get a count of the number of words in a file. You know that there's a command that does it, you just don't know what it is. Try running:

```
% apropos words
look (1) - find words in the system dictionary
canonhdr (8) \- canonicalize case in keywords
wc (1) - count lines, words and characters
```

At the very last line, you see that the *wc* command does what you want—it counts the number of lines, words, and characters in a file.

The success of *apropos* depends on your system administrator having created a special database for each directory tree of manpages, stored in a file called *whatis*. If you get an error message similar to the following:

```
% apropos words
/usr/local/man/whatis: No such file or directory
```

then your administrator has not created the database. Send her email with the full text of the error message.

The *apropos* command is the equivalent of running *man* with the −*k* option.

Quick Reference
of troubleshooting techniques

Information to find and keep

What directories should be in my search path? _____

_____

_____

What value should MANPATH be set to for our

system?_____

What shell do I use? _____

What is the name of my setup file? _____

What terminal type do I use?_____

What terminal type do I use when I log in from home?

_____

Command not found

1. Check that you typed the name of the command correctly. Did you remember a space between the command name and options? Mistake an O for a 0 or I for a 1? Make any needed substitutions, such as a file name for "filename"? Forget something (like a capital letter) or add something (like a command-line prompt such as % or $) that you don't need to type?

2. Check that the command is installed on the system with *whereis*; e.g., to see the full pathname of the *who* command, type:

   % whereis who

3. As a one-time fix, run the program with its full pathname; for example, if the program's full pathname is */usr/bin/who*, type:

   % /usr/bin/who

4. For a permanent fix, use a text editor to add the command's directory to the end of your search path.

Command doesn't act like you expect

1. See if there are two versions of the command with *whereis*:

   % whereis ls
   ls: /usr/5bin/ls /usr/bin/ls

2. Check which version of the command you are running:

   % which ls
   /usr/bin/ls

3. Either set an alias for the preferred path or change the order in which directories are searched.

Can't remember command name

Use *apropos* to search for commands having to do with a key word; e.g., to see the command that has to do with word count, you might try:

   % apropos count

Don't know command options or syntax

Use the *man* command to display and search through the online manual page; e.g., to see a description of the *wc* command, type:

   % man wc

If the *man* command doesn't work, ask your administrator for the values to use in your MANPATH variable.

The program runs, but you get gibberish

The terminal type could be set wrong. Quit out of the program. If you don't know your correct terminal type, ask your administrator. Reset the terminal type. For example, to reset the terminal type to a vt100 terminal, type:

   % setenv TERM vt100

Or:

   % TERM=vt100; export TERM

What you need to know about sharing files

On a UNIX system, your files can be shared with other users.

UNIX is a multiuser system, which means you share it with other users. The files that you read or edit on your terminal can also be seen by your coworkers.

Files are stored on a hard disk that is mounted on the UNIX system. If you and a coworker are both using the same system, then the file */departments/writers/meetings/minutes.txt* that you see on your terminal can also be accessed on your coworker's terminal under the same pathname.

This means that on a UNIX system, you don't have to deal with trading floppy disks to give a file to someone else. You can just tell someone the pathname to the file, and they should be able to find it on the system.

Or at least, that's the theory. In actuality, there are security measures for preventing people from seeing or editing files that you don't want them to. There are also complications with more than one person being able to work on the same files: how do you make sure that you aren't both making changes at the same time?

When sharing files, the sorts of things that you might want to ask your administrator about are:

Permissions can be confusing

It seems like everyone has run into the file permissions "wall" a few times before they understand it. Why can't others read my file? Why can't I save my changes to this file?

Linda Walsh

About filenames

Filenames are case-sensitive

PC and Mac users are used to filenames being case-insensitive; e.g., you can access the file Status under the names STATUS or status. In UNIX, however, filenames are case-sensitive. If you type:

    % ls Status

the ls command will only list a file called *Status*, not *status*, *STATUS*, or any other variation.

Filenames can be any (reasonable) length

PC users are used to having to keep filenames to 8 characters, with an additional 3-character extension (for example, *CHAPTER1.TXT*). Although some older UNIX systems restricted filenames to 14 characters, today all UNIX systems support long filenames. While there is usually a maximum length, it's unlikely you'll ever encounter it.

If you expect to transfer a file to DOS, however, you should name it using the 8.3 convention anyway. Otherwise the filename is truncated when it is transferred to DOS.

Extensions are less important in UNIX

PC users are used to files having a three-character extension identifying the file type. For example, an executable file ends in *.exe*, a text file ends in *.txt*, and a file created by Microsoft Word ends has a *.doc* extension. PCs use these extensions to determine what program to start when you open the file.

On UNIX, filename extensions, or *suffixes*, don't matter as much. Some extensions are still common, but more as a convention than anything else. You create a PostScript file with a *.ps* extension so other people will quickly identify it as a PostScript file, but programs don't depend on that suffix; the *lpr* command will send the file to the printer under any name.

Dots (.) can be used in filenames

Because UNIX doesn't particularly care about extensions, you can use dots in filenames as separation characters. You can use dots to separate parts of a filename for easy reading (for example, *sales.memo* or *ed.answer*).

However, if you think you might be transferring a file between UNIX and PCs, you'll want to avoid using dots, so the filenames won't be garbled when you transfer the file to DOS. If you frequently transfer files to DOS, then use underscores (_) instead of dots (and keep filenames to the 8.3 length restriction).

On UNIX, the only special use of dots in filenames is at the beginning. A file starting with a dot (for example, *.cshrc* or *.profile*) isn't shown when you type ls. These special "dot files" are generally used to configure programs like the shell, editors, mailers, etc.

Some characters are problematic

Several characters cause problems when they appear in UNIX filenames, because of complications with the shell. For that reason, it's uncommon to find files with these characters in their names. Luckily, it is also difficult to create files with these characters. The characters to avoid in filenames include:

- Blank spaces or tabs
- Asterisks (*) and question marks (?)
- Parentheses (), square brackets [], and curly braces {}
- Greater and less than signs <>
- Vertical bars |
- Front and back slashes /\
- Any control character

- Why can't I read a file or list a directory?
- How do I let my coworkers edit my files?
- I made changes to a file, but now I find out that I can't write it. Are my changes lost?
- How can I be sure that no one else is working on this file right now?

This chapter explains the concepts behind sharing files on UNIX and describes how you might deal with these questions in the absence of your system administrator.

Security measures make sure that people aren't reading or editing files that they shouldn't be.

For most of my files, I don't care who sees them. I don't have much to hide. And I also assume that everyone's too busy with their own work to bother with what I'm doing.

But here and there, I have files that are actually important, and which I want to keep under wraps. Even if you don't lock your doors at home, there are probably a few things that you want to protect, such as your great-aunt's diamonds, your childrens' birth certificates, and your ninth-grade love letters.

On a UNIX system, the sorts of things I might want to keep other people from reading are personal mail messages, resumes, embarrassingly bad poetry I've written, and an angry memo that I wisely never sent but held onto anyway. There are also files that I don't mind other people seeing, but I mind them changing, such as my *.cshrc* and *.login* files.

Similarly, there are files on the system that need to be protected from me. For example, if I could see other people's mail files, I might be tempted to read mail between managers about problems with another employee or learn something else that's really none of my business.

Security is needed to prevent damage to the system and to protect the privacy of each user.

For people coming from Macintoshes or PCs

In UNIX, your files and your home directory aren't "on" your terminal. Your files are stored remotely on a central file server.

If you turn off the terminal on your desk, that doesn't mean that your files are protected. Your files are on a server 24 hours a day, available to many people.

The only privacy you have for UNIX files is your trust in other people and on the file permissions and directory permissions for those files.

Sometimes file security gets in the way of what you want to do.

Now and then, you'll need to edit someone else's file, and then you learn that you don't have permission to change it. Or maybe you don't even have permission to read it. Or you may ask someone else to work on a file of yours and then learn that they can't do it. Sometimes, you might need to run a program, but get errors such as "permission denied" or "can't open."

Security always comes at the price of convenience. If you lock your doors, then you have to find a way to get keys to your occasional houseguests. And if you protect your files, then you have to find a way to lend them to the people you work with.

Each UNIX file has its own distinct set of permissions to define who can read, write, or execute the file.

The way that file security works on UNIX systems is that each file has its own set of permissions. These permissions define who on the system can read, write, or *execute* the file.

Being able to read a file is easy to understand: it just means that you can look at the file with a program like *more*, maybe even browse through it using your editor.

Being able to write the file is also easy to understand. It means that you can make changes to the file.

Being able to execute a file is just a fancy way of saying that you can run it as a command.

Each file is owned by a particular user.

When a file is created, it belongs to the user who created it. For example, if I created a new file:

```
% ls hello.out
hello.out not found
% echo "Hello" > hello.out
% ls hello.out
hello.out
```

What you need to know about sharing files

The new file belongs to me. I can confirm this by running the *ls –l* command. Among other things, this command tells me who owns the file:

```
% ls -l hello.out
-rw-r----- 1 lmui 6 Nov 16 10:46 hello.out
```

The part to pay attention to is that the third field in the listing reads "lmui," which is my login name. This tells me and anyone else that the *hello.out* file belongs to me.

This matters for the following reasons:

- The permissions on the file are initially set by the owner's environment

- Only the owner of the file and the superuser can change the permissions on the file

Each file is assigned to a particular "group" of users.

When a new file is created, the file isn't just assigned an owner. It's also assigned a *group.*

The best way to think about groups is as collections of users. For example, *sales* might be the collection of the users who work in the sales department, and *prod* might be the group of people who work in the production department. All the managers in a company might belong to a group called *mgrs.* And on most systems, a special group, *wheel,* is assigned to users who can perform some system administration tasks.

On many UNIX systems, each user can belong to more than one group. The manager of the sales department would belong to both the *sales* and *mgrs* group. On some systems, each user belongs to all his or her groups at all times. On other systems, you only belong to one group at a time and must explicitly change groups whenever you want to switch your membership.

Use ls –lg to find out to what group a file belongs.

On some versions of UNIX, typing *ls –l* shows you who owns the file, but not the name of the group that the file belongs to. To see the name of the group, run *ls –lg* on the file.

```
% ls -lg ch01
```

Administrators can see all files on the system

Regardless of the permissions on a file, you can't hide it from your system administrator. Your administrator can read, edit, or delete all files on the system.

In general, administrators stay out of your personal files. They respect your privacy, and they also have much more important things to do. Most administrators will only look into private areas if they have to—for example, if files are corrupted or if they notice suspicious activity that might endanger the system.

```
total 396
-rw-r-----  1 lois sales 95232 Oct 20 11:48 ch01
```

You'll see that after the name of the owner (*lois*) is the name of the group, in this case *sales*.

On System V–derived versions of UNIX, the group is automatically shown with *ls –l*. If your *ls –l* shows groups automatically, then you don't need to supply the *g* option.

You can find out to what groups a user belongs.

To find out what groups someone belongs to, use the *groups* command. For example, if I wanted to know what groups I belong to, I could run the *groups* command with no arguments:

```
% groups
ora staff book dmg
```

I belong to the groups *ora*, *staff*, *book*, and *dmg*.

To find out the groups that another user belongs to, type their login name as an argument to the *groups* command:

```
% groups frank
frank: ora prod editors book
```

On some systems (BSD–based systems), you belong to all your groups all the time. That is, Frank can access a file that belongs to *prod* and then another file that belongs to *editors* without having to change anything. On other systems, you can only belong to one group at a time, and you have to use the *newgrp* command to change groups (and possibly also type in a password for the new group).

Only the system administrator can add or delete users from a group.

Each file has three separate sets of permissions: for the owner of the file, the group, and everyone else.

For each file, read, write, and execute permissions are assigned in three separate sets:

- Permissions for the owner (user) of the file
- Permissions for the group that the file belongs to

- Permissions for all others

Whether or not you can read, write, or execute a file depends on which of these sets you belong to: whether you own the file, belong to its group, or fall into the band of riffraff known as "other."

If you don't have read permission, you won't be able to see the contents of the file.

If you try to open a file that you don't have read permission for, you won't be able to see the contents of the file. For example, if you use *vi* or Emacs or *more* or any other UNIX program to see a file that is restricted from you, the program will fail and will give an error message such as "Permission denied" or "cannot open."

```
% more who.out
who.out: Permission denied
```

Just because you can read a file doesn't mean that you can change it.

If you do have read permission for a file, you may still not be able to edit it. For example, the */etc/passwd* file on your system is one that all users can read, but only your system administrator can edit it.

When you have read but not write permission for a file, the file is opened "read-only." You can open the file in an editor and even make changes within the editor; but if you try to save those changes to the file, you won't be able to write the file.

Directory permissions refer to the ability to list the files or create new files.

As far as UNIX is concerned, directories are just special files. Only instead of containing text or data or what-have-you, directories just contain pointers to other files, and the operating system pulls a few magic tricks to make us think of directories as "containing" these files.

File permission metaphor

You might think of the UNIX file permissions like an apartment building that you live in. There are common areas that everyone in the building has access to—the hallways, the laundry room, etc. That's:

rw-rw-rw-

Then there's your apartment, which you share with your family or roommates:

rw-rw----

And then there's your room, which is yours alone:

rw-------

ALL
x 1 —
3 1 2
r 1 4
√ for files
√ for directory

GROUP
x 1 —
3 1 2
r 1 4
default = 777
default = 666

OWNER
x 1 —
3 1 2
r 1 4

So the same way that write permission to a file determines whether you can change the file, write permission to a directory determines whether you can change the contents of the directory; that is, whether you can add new files or delete existing files. Similarly, read permission for a directory determines whether you can list the contents of the directory via *ls* or another program. Meanwhile, execute permission controls whether you can *cd* to the directory.

The directory permissions don't have any effect on the permissions of the files within it. You might not have read or write permission for a directory, but you might still be able to read and write a file within it (assuming you know its pathname ahead of time and don't need to *ls* for it!). Also, since the read and write permissions don't affect the execute permissions, it is possible that you might be able to *cd* to a directory that you can't read.

Use ls –l to learn the permissions on a file.

When you type *ls –l* on a file, you'll see the file's permissions represented in the first column. For example:

```
% ls -l ch01
-rw-r-----  1 lmui        68608 Oct 18 13:11 ch01
```

The first column of this listing is a 10-character string consisting of dashes and the characters r, w, and x. This string represents the permissions for each file. To interpret the permissions, you need to break up this string into four distinct parts.

The first character tells you what kind of file this is, and doesn't have much to do with file permissions. When it's a –, it means that the file is a regular file. Other values are d for a directory and l for a symbolic link.

You can ignore the first character for now. The remaining nine characters represent who has read, write, or execute permission for the file. Think of it as consisting of three sets each of the characters r, w, x, and –. The first set represents owner permission, the second set represents group permission, and the third set represents permissions for everyone else (aka "the world").

An r represents read permission, w represents write permission, and x represents execute permission. For each set, the three characters rwx always appear in order. If any of these characters is missing (i.e., replaced by a dash), then that permission is denied.

When the file called *ch01* shows permissions -rw-r-----, this means that the owner of the file (*lmui*) can read and write the file, members of the file's group can only read the file, and everyone else is left out in the cold.

You'll find that r, w, and x aren't the only letters you'll see in a file's permissions. Occasionally you'll see the special characters s, S, t, and T in place of x. This means that the file or directory has special permissions; in general, only administrators concern themselves with this level of permissions.

Use ls –ld to see the permissions for a directory.

When you run *ls –l* on a directory, you see the permissions of all the files within the directory. For example, if I type *ls –l* on the *tmp* subdirectory of my home directory, I'll only see a listing of the files within *tmp*:

```
% ls -l ~/tmp
total 280
-r--r--r--  1 lmui 276480 Jul 18 09:21 ch01.tmp
-r--r--r--  1 lmui 115345 Jul 18 11:51 ch02.tmp
```

Sometimes you don't want to see the files within the directory; you just want to see just the permissions on the directory itself. For that you should specify the *–d* command-line option as well. With the *ls –ld* command, you'll see the permissions on the directory itself, not on its contents.

```
% ls -ld ~/tmp
drwxr-x--x  2 lmui 512 Aug 25 17:32 /home/lmui/tmp
```

This tells you that the directory *tmp* in my home directory is read/write to myself and read-only for my group. It cannot be read or written by anyone else; however, all users can *cd* to the directory, since it is executable for all. The initial d means that it's a directory.

What do you do when you need permissions changed on a file?

When I have a problem with permissions, the first thing I do is see who owns the file. Then I ask the person via email or telephone to give me permission.

I need permissions changed most often when an author or editor tells me I can start working on their files, and I find that I don't have permission for any of them. One suggestion I have is before you ask someone to change permissions on a file, check to see if there are other files that need to be changed too. Otherwise you end up sending a dozen messages and waiting each time, rather than getting them all changed at once.

Ellen Siever

If you need permissions changed, you can ask the owner of the file or the system administrator.

It happens now and then that you need to read or change a file, and you don't have permission to do so. You need the permissions changed, and only two people can do that: the owner and the system administrator.

In general, you should always try to get the owner of the file to help you before you try to find the administrator. The reason is that the owner is likely to know what the file is for and who should actually have access to it. Administrators are unlikely to be familiar with every file on the system and may therefore be wary about giving you permission without first consulting the owner.

The owner of a file can extend read and write permission to all users.

If you own a file, you can give read permission to other users on the system using the *chmod* command. For example, to give read permission to all users, the owner can type:

```
% chmod a+r filename
```

where *filename* is the name of the file or directory that you want to others to be able to read. The syntax a+r says to add read (r) permission to all (a) users.

You can also give write permission to other users using the *chmod* command. To give write permission to all users, the owner can type:

```
% chmod a+w filename
```

where *filename* is the name of the file or directory that you want to others to be able to write. As with a+r, the syntax a+w says to give write (w) permission to all (a) users.

You can also give both read and write permission in one command, like this:

```
% chmod a+rw filename
```

The owner of a file can extend read and write permission to just the group.

You may not want to give all users permission to read a file. If you only want to give permission to other people in the file's group, you can use the g+r syntax instead:

```
% chmod g+r filename
```

Instead of giving permission to all users (a), you are giving permission to just the group (g). Similarly, you can give write permission to others in the group with g+w:

```
% chmod g+w filename
```

and both read and write permission with g+rw:

```
% chmod g+rw filename
```

For example, suppose my coworker Mike wants to edit a file of mine called *updates*. I can let him do this by giving read and write permission to the world with *chmod a+r*, but it's safer to give permission only to members of the file's group, if you can.

If I run *ls –lg* on *updates*, I'll see that it belongs to the group *prod*, but is read/write only to the owner, *lmui* (me).

```
% ls -lg updates
-rw-------  1 lmui prod 249 Oct 25 09:24 updates
```

I can check that Mike belongs to the *prod* group by using the *groups* command:

```
% groups mike
mike : ora prod
```

So I don't have to give read and write permission to the entire world, just to the group:

```
% chmod g+rw updates
```

Now Mike and other users in the group *prod* can read and write the file.

The owner of a file can change the group that the file belongs to.

If you own a file or directory, you can change the group that it belongs to. You might do this if you want to extend access to someone who belongs to a different group, without having to extend access to the world.

juicy.gossip

The only files that I've paid attention to the security on were personnel files when I was a manager.

I don't restrict file permissions much. However, I have been known to label a sensitive memo with a misleading or obscure name. No sense in leaving a file around labelled juicy.gossip.

Linda Lamb

To change the group for a file or directory, use the *chgrp* command. For example, suppose my coworker Frank wants access to one of my files, called *updates*. The file is read/writable by its group, but belongs to the group *prod*:

```
% ls -lg updates
-rw-rw----  1 lmui prod 590 Sep  8 10:20 updates
```

I check and see that Frank doesn't belong to the group *prod*:

```
% groups frank
frank : mgrs book ora
```

I can give read/write permission to the world, but it's better to restrict it to a group. I change the file to the group *book*, which both of us belong to:

```
% chgrp book updates
% ls -lg updates
-rw-rw----  1 lmui book 590 Sep  8 10:20 updates
```

Now Frank and all other members of the *book* group can read and write my file, but the file is still restricted from "outsiders." (In this example, users who belong to *prod,* but not to *book,* can no longer read or write the file.)

You can also remove permissions.

In addition to adding permissions, you can also remove permissions. For example, if you own a file and want to remove read and write permission from the group, you can use *chmod g–rw*:

```
% chmod g-rw filename
```

You can change permissions for all files in a directory.

What if you want to change permissions for a lot of files? For example, suppose you want to extend read/write access to your group, for all files in the directory.

Of course, one thing you can do is to run *chmod* on all of them individually. You can also use the wildcard character (*) to change all files in the directory:

```
% chmod g+rw *
```

The problem with this is that you won't change any files in subdirectories. For example, suppose you're in your home directory, and you have a *Mail* subdirectory in your home

What you need to know about sharing files

directory. Running *chmod* would change the permissions to all the files in your home directory:

```
% ls -1
total 26
drwxr-x--x 2 lmui 512 Dec 14 17:54 Mail
-rw-r----- 1 lmui 20181 Dec 14 17:54 mbox
-rw-r----- 1 lmui 867 Dec 14 17:54 people
-rw------- 1 lmui 249 Dec 14 17:54 updates
% chmod g+rw *
% ls -1
total 26
drwxrwx--x 2 lmui 512 Dec 14 17:54 Mail
-rw-rw---- 1 lmui 20181 Dec 14 17:54 mbox
-rw-rw---- 1 lmui 867 Dec 14 17:54 people
-rw-rw---- 1 lmui 249 Dec 14 17:54 updates
```

However, files in the *Mail* subdirectory remain unchanged.

```
% ls -1 Mail
total 184
-rw------- 1 lmui 105808 Dec 14 17:54 lamb
-rw------- 1 lmui 37010 Dec 14 17:54 tim
-rw------- 1 lmui 35184 Dec 14 17:54 val
```

Luckily, there's a command-line option for changing permissions in subdirectories (*recursively*). You can use the *–R* option to *chmod* to change the permissions for all subdirectories. For example:

```
% chmod -R g+rw *
```

You can "become" another user to gain their privileges.

In the absence of having another user change permissions, another way you can get permission to a file is to log in as that user. Of course, you can only do this if you know the other user's password.

To become another user, use the *su* command. The *su* command is the same one that administrators use to become the superuser. However, it isn't just for a superuser: *su* stands for "switch user," and can be used to become any other user.

For example, if *lois* knows *jimmy*'s password, she can type:

```
% su jimmy
Password:
```

You can give yourself permission

The owner of a file can also add or subtract permissions for him- or herself. For example:

```
% chmod u+rw who.out
```

This command gives the owner read/write permissions for the file called who.out. The letter u represents the owner (user), and +rw adds read and write permission.

Usually, you automatically have read/write permission for files you own— but not always (for example, if the file was transferred from somewhere else).

Once she types in Jimmy's password correctly, Lois can work as if she were Jimmy. Lois's prompt may not have changed, but as far as UNIX is concerned, she is working as Jimmy. For example, if she creates a new file, the new file will belong to *jimmy*.

Although you can do whatever you want as Jimmy, you should respect his privacy. Don't start looking at his personal files. And rather than edit files as Jimmy, you should instead just change the permissions, so you can become yourself again and make changes as yourself. To get back to being yourself, just type *exit* or CTRL-D.

Of course, you should only use *su* to become another user if you have that user's permission to do so at your discretion. And be aware that a record of your activity is stored online, so it's not as if no one will ever find out. If you looked in */usr/adm/messages*, you would see:

```
Nov 18 14:54:25 ruby su: 'su jimmy' succeeded for lois on /
dev/ttyre
```

You should also be sure to send the other user some email telling them that you used their password and changed some files:

```
% mail jimmy
Subject: changed permission on ch01

After you left last night, I needed to edit ch01 so I did
"su jimmy" and changed permissions on it. Hope you don't
mind. Thanks,

Lois
```

Only the administrator can legitimately change the ownership of a file.

Sometimes, the best way to resolve a problem with permissions is to simply give someone else ownership of a file. For example, if you give up responsibility for maintaining a file, the new person who takes over should really be the one who owns the file.

When you need to change ownership of a file, you need to ask the system administrator. Only the administrator can explicitly change who owns a file, using the *chown* command.

What you need to know about sharing files

There is also a bit syntax for changing permissions

There are two types of syntax for chmod. In this chapter, we describe things using the "addition and subtraction" syntax, such as g+w to add write permission to a group. This is confusing in itself, but there is also another syntax to chmod which is even more elaborate, using a special "bit syntax."

Bit syntax is based on binary arithmetic. For each of the three sections of the permissions string, you can assign a number from 0 to 7:

- 0 means no permission. In an *ls –l* listing, it would be represented as ---.

- 1 means execute permission only. In an *ls –l* listing, it would be --x.

- 2 means write permission only. In an *ls –l* listing, it would be -w-. (This is very uncommon.)

- 4 means read permission only. In an *ls –l* listing, it would be r--.

You can also add permissions as needed:

- 5 means read and execute permission (4+1). In an *ls –l* listing, this would be r-x.

- 6 means read and write permission (4+2). In an *ls –l* listing, this would be rw-.

- 7 means all permissions (4+2+1). In an *ls –l* listing, this would be rwx.

You can also theoretically use 3 for write and execute permission (-wx), but this is very uncommon.

Using these digits, you can express permissions as a 3-digit string. Permissions of 664 mean that the file has read/write permissions for the owner and group, and only read permission for everyone else—i.e., permissions -rw-rw-r--. 640 means that the file has read and write permissions for the owner, read-only permission for the group, and no permissions for others (i.e. -rw-r----). 777 means that everyone can do everything (i.e., -rwxrwxrwx)

In general, this syntax for defining permissions is most useful for expert users who understand all the implications of what they are doing.

If you can read a file but can't write it, you can copy the file and make your changes in the copy.

If you need to change a read-only file, what you should do is find the owner of the file and have its permissions changed. But if you can't find the owner of the file, and your changes really must be done immediately, you can also just copy the file and make your changes in the copy:

```
% cp updates ~/updates.mine
% vi ~/updates.mine
(edit as needed)
```

The only caveat is that you need to make sure that your "new" version of the file is copied over the "real" version before more changes are made to it. So send email to the owner:

```
% mail mike
Subject: updates file

Hey, I needed to make changes to updates, but I didn't have
write permission, so I made my changes into a copy in my
home directory named updates.mine. Please stay out of the
updates file for now. I'll let you know when the changed
version can be copied into the original.
```

Otherwise you risk having to merge changes from two different versions of the file.

If you have already made edits when you learn the file is read-only, you can still save your changes.

Sometimes you don't find out that you lack the permission to change a file until you've already made changes in the editor. When you open a read-only file for editing, you usually see some indication that the file is read-only. For example, in *vi*, you'll see this message at the bottom of the screen:

```
"who.out" [Read only] 57 lines, 2742 characters
```

But you might not always notice the messages before you start making changes. The first time you find out that the file isn't writable is when you try to save changes:

```
"who.out" File is read only
```

What you need to know about sharing files

And when you try to quit, you'll find out that your changes haven't been saved:

```
No write since last change (:quit! overrides)
```

It looks as if your changes are lost. But they don't have to be.

One thing you can do is save your changes under a different filename. For example:

```
:w ~/tmp
```

Then quit out of *vi* and have the permissions on the file changed. Once the permissions are fixed, you can copy the *tmp* file back over the original, and your changes have been saved.

If you own the file, you can save the changes without exiting the editor. First run a subshell to use *chmod* to change permissions:

```
:!chmod u+w %
```

(In *vi*, % can be used to represent the name of the file.)

Then write the file using w! (The exclamation point is needed to make sure that the changes take place. Even though you changed permissions on the file, *vi* thinks the file is still read-only, because it was read-only when the file was originally opened.)

```
:w!
```

Sometimes several users have to work on several sets of files at once.

At our office, we produce books. At the final stage of a book's production, several people might be editing the files at the same time: one is entering index entries, another is fixing page breaks, and a third is entering last-minute changes from the author.

When things are going smoothly, we all know what each other is doing, and we stay out of each other's files. But occasionally there are conflicts.

chmod 700

My file permissions are set to be open. Anyone can read, write, or execute anything.

There are only a few files where I want more privacy. I learned "chmod 700" for those files. Then, only I can get into them.

Carol Vogt

The initial permissions of a file are determined by the user who creates it

A file initially belongs to the person who created it

The permissions for a file depends on whoever originally created the file:

- The person who owns the file is the person who created it.
- The group that the file belongs to is the user's *default group*.
- The initial permissions on the file are set by the user's *umask value*.

Each user has a default group

Each user has a default group. This is the group that a file belongs to when you first create it.

Your default group is set by your system administrator in your passwd entry. See Chapter 2 for information on how to see your passwd entry. The default group ID appears as the fourth field in the passwd entry—for example, my entry reads:

```
lmui:ctA1223xqXp/Q:183:100:Linda Mui:/home/lmui:/bin/tcsh
```

In this case, my default group ID is 100. To find out what group 100 corresponds to, look in the system's group database. If your system supports NIS (aka Yellow Pages), then you can see the group database by typing:

```
% ypcat group
```

Otherwise, just look in the file /etc/group. In our group database, you'll see that group 100 corresponds to the group called ora:

```
ora:*:100:root,sybase
```

If I create a new file, I'll find that it belongs to group ora.

The initial permissions for new files are set by your umask value

Every user has a value called a *umask*. The best way to think about your umask is to imagine that, left to their own devices, all new files are created read/write to everyone—that is, with the permissions -rw-rw-rw-, or permissions 666.

Making a file read/write to everyone isn't always the best idea. So the umask command can be used to "mask out" parts of those permissions, based on chmod's bit syntax.

Like chmod's bit syntax, umask values are given as a 3-digit string, which is subtracted from the default 666 permissions. For example, a umask of 002 means that the default permissions will be 666-002 = 664, or read/write for the owner and group and read-only for everyone else. All new files are now created with permissions -rw-rw-r--.

By default, the umask value is set to 022—so all files you create are read/write to you and read-only to everyone else (i.e. permissions 644, or -rw-r--r--).

umask is generally run in your .cshrc or .profile file. For example:

```
umask 066
```

This means that all newly created files will have permissions 600, i.e. read/write for owner and no access for anyone else.

What you need to know about sharing files

It's dangerous if two people edit a file at the same time.

The danger when multiple users are using the same files is that if two people edit a file at the same time, the file is guaranteed to be corrupted.

Remember that a file remains unchanged until you write it. So suppose I open a file for writing in *vi,* and I start editing away.

Now suppose that my friend Mike wants to edit the same file and doesn't know I'm already using it. UNIX doesn't tell him that someone else is already using the file: instead, he can open it in his own editor and make changes. But since I haven't written my changes yet, the version of the file that Mike opens in his editor is exactly the one I originally opened, *without my changes.*

I finish my changes, write the file, and quit the editor. Then Mike finishes his changes, writes the file, and quits his editor. Only, since the version of the file Mike was working on didn't include my changes, all my changes are now lost.

So when several users are working together, they must be sure that others aren't editing files before they start making changes. Otherwise someone is certain to be "crunched."

There are systems for making sure that two people aren't editing the same file.

There are two systems for controlling projects that are worked on by multiple users: RCS (Revision Control System) and SCCS (Source Code Control System). We aren't going to tell you much about them, but you should understand a little about how they work.

Both RCS and SCCS are designed for maintaining edits to a file. The idea is that the revision system keeps a record of what changes were made to a file and when, so that if you ever want to revert to a previous version you can do it easily. For programmers, this is very important, since today's changes might introduce new bugs and the only way to fix it is to revert to a previous version. You can also see a list of differences between two versions of a file, to help you figure out exactly where things went wrong.

RCS and SCCS also give users a way to "lock" a file. By locking a file, you declare that you're making changes to the file, and no one else better touch it. Locking a file is also called "checking out" a file.

By using RCS or SCCS, you can not only maintain your files, but also ensure that only one user is editing them at the same time.

Under RCS or SCCS, the archive containing all versions of the file is maintained in a separate file, usually in an *RCS* or *SCCS* subdirectory. You may not even see a copy of the file in the main directory. If you do see a copy of the file, you won't have write permission to the file unless you have "locked" the file for editing.

RCS and SCCS are complex systems, too complex to cover in detail here. However, if you have either RCS or SCCS installed on your system, you should be sure to learn how to use it, since it is one of the safest ways for multiple users to share files.

Quick Reference
to file sharing

"Permission denied."

If this error appears when you try to read the file, you don't have read permission. If the error appears as you try to save the file, you don't have write permission:

1. See who owns the file:

   % ls -l filename

2. Ask the owner for read/write permission.

3. If the owner isn't available, ask your system administrator to change the file permissions.

4. If you have read permission, you can copy the file into your own directory and work on it there; e.g., to copy a file named memo to your own directory:

   % cp memo ~/memo.mine

   Be sure to tell the owner that you made changes to a copy of the file.

Repeated denial to files that you think you should be able to share

1. See what group can read/write the files:

   % ls -lg filenames

2. See what groups you are a member of:

   % groups

3. If you are not a member of the group with permission, ask the file owner to change the group to one you belong to or ask your system administrator to add you to the group.

Can't create or remove files in a directory

1. Check directory permissions on the directory:

   % ls -ld directory

2. Ask the directory's owner to give you permission:

How to change permissions

1. Check the file's permissions, owner, and group:

   % ls -lg

2. If you are the file's owner, use chmod. E.g., to add write permission to all for a file named memo:

   % chmod a+w memo

To add permissions for all users:

   % chmod a+r memo   *read permission*
   % chmod a+w memo   *write permission*
   % chmod a+rw memo *read/write*

To add permissions for the group:

   % chmod g+r memo   *read permission*
   % chmod g+w memo   *write permission*
   % chmod g+rw memo *read/write*

You can also subtract permissions:

   % chmod g-rw memo

Or change permissions on all files in a directory:

   % chmod g+rw *

Or change the group that a file belongs to:

   % chgrp sales memo

3. Or you can use a three-digit number to indicate what permissions you want for a file; e.g., to give read/write permission to both the file owner (you) and to the group of the file memo, type:

   % chmod 660 memo

Other possible values for read-only permission:

   400 -r--------
   440 -r--r-----
   444 -r--r--r--

Read-write:

   600 -rw-------
   660 -rw-rw----
   666 -rw-rw-rw-

Read-write-execute:

   700 -rwx------
   770 -rwxrwx---
   777 -rwxrwxrwx

Execute only:

   100 ---x------
   110 ---x--x---
   111 ---x--x--x

What you need to know about sharing files

CHAPTER 5

What you need to know about printing

Printing is a multistep process for the computer.

Most of the time, printing happens automatically in the background, at the click of a Print button, or with a simple print command. When printing doesn't work, however, any part of the process could be broken. A few basic concepts and tools let you do most of your own troubleshooting on printing.

Regardless of what you're printing, the print process has the same series of steps:

- A file is translated into a language that printers recognize (e.g., PostScript).
- The file is queued to a target printer.
- The job moves to the top of the queue of print jobs.
- The printer prints the file.

This chapter first gives you background on printing on UNIX, describes file formats and how to convert to PostScript, and then gets into troubleshooting what can go wrong.

If a file doesn't print, don't just send it again

Even though I know better, if a file doesn't print when I send it, I sometimes run the same print command again. This is akin to speaking LOUDER to someone who doesn't speak your language; the volume doesn't help.

Arsenio Santos

Print jobs are sent to the printer by a printer daemon.

When you print a file on UNIX, the file doesn't go directly to the printer. Instead, the file is *spooled* for the printer and placed on a queue. You can think of the print spool as a sort of waiting room, where your job patiently sits until it is called to the printer.

The program that determines when a file can be sent from the queue to the printer is called the *printer daemon*. A daemon is a special UNIX program that remains running all the time, waiting for requests. The printer daemon is responsible for determining when a print job is completed and then sending the next job in the queue. If you think of the print spool as the waiting room, then you can think of the printer daemon as the receptionist who yells, "Next!"

Printing works differently depending on whether you use System V or BSD UNIX.

Printing is one of the areas where UNIX systems diverge the most. As we mentioned in Chapter 3, there are two separate camps of UNIX systems, those that are System V–based and those that are BSD–based. Most of the differences between System V and BSD are hidden to the user: for the most part, the only differences a user will see are different command-line options and, occasionally, different output. When it comes to printing, however, BSD and System V UNIX use a completely different spooling method, and a completely different set of commands.

Don't be confused if you see that both sets of commands work on your system, e.g., if you can print files using both *lp* and *lpr*. It's common for modern UNIX systems to support both, so users migrating from one system to another don't have that steep a learning curve. Since they do the same thing, it doesn't matter which commands you use: just use the ones you're most comfortable with.

Files need to be translated into a format that printers recognize.

Files on a computer may be stored in any number of formats. For example, a word processor might save a file in its own special format (such as RTF), or a graphics program might keep files in a format like TIFF or GIF. Sometimes you may even edit a file in a markup language (for example, *troff* or *TeX*). Many files (for example, mail files) are kept in a no-frills text format, sometimes known as ASCII format.

Printers don't understand all of these formats. Printers have their own internal languages to tell them where to place characters, how to draw pictures, when to eject the current page, etc.

On UNIX, most printers use the PostScript standard.

On UNIX systems, the most common printers use the PostScript page description language. PostScript is used because it is a "standard," meaning (in this case) that it is supported by multiple vendors.

This means that when you send a file to a PostScript printer, the file has to be written in PostScript. When you print a file that's in another format, such as a *troff* file or a mail file or whatever, the file needs to somehow be converted into PostScript before anything else happens.

A PostScript file has a unique header.

If you looked at a PostScript file with a text editor or with the *more* command, the start of the file might look like:

```
%!PS-Adobe-2.0
%%Creator: O'Reilly 2.1
%%CreationDate: 12/12/94 14/12/40
%%End Comments
/ld {load def} bind def
/s /stroke ld /f /fill ld /m /moveto ld /l /lineto ld /c /
curveto ld /rgb {255 div 3 1 roll 255 div 3 1 roll 255 div 3
1 roll setrgbcolor} def 126 142 translate
360.0000 508.8000 scale
/picstr 19 string def
152 212 1[152 0 0 -212 0 212]{currentfile picstr
readhexstring pop} image
```

X users may be able to preview PostScript files

If you have a graphical terminal (like an X terminal), you may be able to "preview" files before you actually print them to a printer. By previewing a file, you can see on your screen exactly what will appear on the printer.

The advantage of previewing files is that you can save paper and also save a trip across the hall to the printer room. For many people, previewing comes in most useful when fine-tuning a document. If all you're doing is tweaking a figure until it's placed perfectly on a page, then you may need to repeatedly change the source file, print, and walk to the printer to see what it looks like, over and over again until you get it right. Being able to preview files doesn't take the place of a true WYSIWYG editor, but it does save that portion of the carpet between your desk and the printer.

Files have different formats

Before any file can be printed, it must be converted into PostScript. How this is done depends on what sort of file it is, and how you have things configured at your site.

Text files

A text file is the most familiar and most universal file format. Text files are exactly what they sound like. They do not allow for any formatting, such as italics or changing font size; the files are just plain text. When you save a mail message, it is usually in text format. Also, files that are meant to be read online, such as README files or other notes for users, are written in text format. Text files are sometimes called "ASCII files," because they are formatted entirely using ASCII characters. The following is an example of a text file:

```
**** README ****
To run the programs in this directory:
o If you use the C shell, run the command "source sourceme"
o If you use the Bourne shell, run the command ". dotme"
```

To print a text file, you must convert it into PostScript first. The way this is done is system-specific. You might have a command on your system called enscript that converts text into PostScript. You might have some other command on your system that converts text into PostScript. Or, your administrator might also have set up your printers so that you can send a text file directly to the printer with lpr and the file is converted into PostScript as needed.

troff and TeX files

troff and TeX files are text files interspersed with formatting instructions. The formatting instructions let you indicate italics, spacing, point sizes, fonts, and even primitive drawing commands.

Since troff and TeX files are technically text files, you could print them the same way you print text files, but what you'd get would be exactly what you see on the screen, with all the special codes embedded. This may be readable, but certainly isn't ideal. Instead, to print a troff or TeX file, you should run the file through a different command that interprets the markup codes and converts them into something the printer will understand (i.e., PostScript).

In actuality, printing troff and TeX files usually involves more than one command: first there is a command that converts the troff or TeX code into an intermediary format, and then another command is run that converts the intermediary format into PostScript. In addition, there are often preprocessors for troff files, such as tbl. These preprocessors are needed for converting more complicated structures, such as tables and graphics, into troff.

So to print a troff file, you might have to run a complicated sequence of commands, such as:

```
tbl letter.mm | troff -mm -Tps | devps | lpr
```

This is a simplified version of a command line needed to print troff, and it's already a mouthful. At many sites, administrators prefer to hide these commands from the users. So users are likely to never run these commands directly, but instead run a shell script or Makefile that does the right thing for them. The local command that the user actually types might be format or roffit or just print.

Graphics files

There are many different graphics formats. And for the most part, you can't recognize them from looking at them, because they usually appear in binary format.

The best way to identify a graphics file is from its suffix. A suffix like .gif or .tiff or .xwd is a dead give-away for the GIF, TIFF, or X Window Dump formats. Also look for files with suffixes of .xbm (X bitmap), .xpm (X pixmap), .jpg (JPEG format), etc.

Once you have identified one of these files, though, how do you print it? If you've been paying attention, then you should have guessed by now that what you need to do is convert the file into PostScript and then send it to the printer via *lpr*. So how do you convert it into PostScript?

Well, it really depends on what you have installed on your system. There are many different packages for converting graphics files, but there are none that are standard on all systems.

One popular package is the pbmplus package. To print a *GIF* file with pbmplus, you need to run several commands to convert it to PostScript. For example:

```
giftoppm tapir.gif | pnmtops | lpr
```

Another package that works this way is ImageMagick.

You may also be able to convert the graphics file through a graphics program. *xv* is an example of a shareware graphics program that you can use to view many different types of graphics files and then save them under a variety of formats, including PostScript.

Know your suffixes

Often, the suffix of the file tells you what sort of file it is. The following are common suffixes:

- *.ps*— PostScript
- *.eps*—Encapsulated PostScript

- *.txt*—Text file
- *.mm, .ms, .me, .man, .roff – troff* file (*–m** suffix denotes the *troff* macro package to use. For example, a file with a *.mm* suffix should be formatted with the *–mm* option to *troff*).
- *.tex*—*TeX* file
- *.gif, .tiff, .bm, .xbm, .xwd, .jpg*—Various graphics formats

Finding out the kind of file

You can also use the *file* command to learn the formats of files. For example:

```
% file *
```

Although file suffixes are not as important in UNIX as they are for PC users, there are naming conventions that can tell you the type of file. The following are common suffixes:

ch06-space.fm:	Frame Maker document
ch06-space.fm.lck:	ASCII text
ch06-space.ps:	PostScript document
glossary:	[nt]roff, tbl, or eqn input text
qreftest:	Shell commands

file doesn't recognize all file formats. It also does a lot of guessing. But all in all, it's a handy tool for figuring out what kind of file you have.

No fear, you don't have to learn how to write this nonsense. Your applications create the PostScript files for you, and you hardly ever need to even see the PostScript code. It's just a good idea to be able to recognize PostScript when you see it.

Often, PostScript filenames have a suffix of *.ps* (for example, *chapter1.ps*). Files containing a more specialized format of Post-Script, called *encapsulated postscript*, often have names with the suffix *.eps*.

The lpr or lp command prints PostScript files. Other commands are needed to translate and print other kinds of files.

The way to print a PostScript file on your system depends on what kind of UNIX system you have. On System V–derived systems, use the *lp* command:

```
% lp chapter1.ps
```

On BSD–derived systems, use the *lpr* command:

```
% lpr chapter1.ps
```

The *lp* or *lpr* command sends the file directly to the print spooler. Since the file is already in PostScript, it does not need to be translated before it can be sent to the printer. When printing a file in any other format, the computer needs to first convert it into PostScript and then call *lpr* or *lp*.

If a file doesn't print, the problem might be the PostScript file.

When a file doesn't print, you need to first figure out if the problem is with the PostScript file itself.

First of all, if only part of the file prints, then something is probably wrong with the file itself or the application that created it. You can check by sending the file to the printer a second time; if it stops at the same point, then the file is the problem.

Look for error messages. For example, one of the following error messages:

```
lpr: standard input: empty input file
```

or

```
lp: ERROR: No (or empty) input files.
```

tells you that the application failed to send PostScript output to *lpr* or *lp*. The problem is with your application or the source file itself.

Failing error messages, the next thing is to try saving the file as PostScript. The way you save the file as PostScript depends on the application.

Once you have the PostScript file, you can make sure it's legitimate PostScript by looking for a line like this at the top of the file:

```
%!PS-Adobe-2.0 EPSF-1.2
```

If you don't see a line like this, then your application did not generate PostScript. (The "%!" string is the only necessary part of that line; the remainder of the line, starting with "PS-Adobe," is just a comment.)

Even if the file is genuine PostScript, there may still be something wrong with it. For example, it might be a PostScript file that doesn't actually have any pages. This might happen if you try printing a range of pages that doesn't exist in a document (for example, pages 10-12 in an 8-page report). The resulting PostScript file will have a legitimate PostScript header, but no actual body text.

If you don't see anything wrong yourself, you might try asking if other people are having trouble printing to that printer. Or try sending a short PostScript file that you have printed successfully in the past to that printer. This will tell you whether something is wrong with the printer. If other jobs print fine, then something is wrong with your file.

Be aware that sometimes a bad file can "hang" a printer, requiring it to be rebooted before it can print again. So even if other print jobs are also failing to print at that printer, something may still be wrong with your file. Reboot the printer and then send a PostScript file that has worked in the past. If it doesn't print, then something is seriously wrong with the printer, with your printer daemon, or with your network, and your system administrator should be informed. If it does print, then send your "corrupted" file and cross your fingers that it works this time. If it doesn't, something's wrong with your application or source file.

Not all PostScript printers are the same

Each printer has its own PostScript interpreter. Not all PostScript interpreters are equal.

At our site, we have a printer that we got for a very good price, but its PostScript interpreter is less than perfect. (We named the printer moa.) So occasionally, we send print jobs to moa that don't print, but which would work fine on other printers. It isn't because anything's wrong with the file, but because the printer itself isn't up to snuff. So when something doesn't print, it sometimes helps to try out a different printer to make sure it's the file that's at fault and not the printer.

Another possibility is that not all PostScript interpreters are equal, and your PostScript file may not be compatible with that printer's interpreter. If you have another PostScript printer manufactured by a different vendor, you might try that printer instead.

Although most of a PostScript file is incomprehensible, you can sometimes read page counts.

With many PostScript files, you can often look at the PostScript file to find out how many pages it contains. For example, you may see this line near the end of a file:

%%Pages: 21

This tells you that there are 21 pages total in the file. I frequently use the *tail* command on PostScript files to see how many pages to expect:

```
% tail ch00.ps
    . . .
%%Pages: 5
```

(The *tail* command shows the last ten lines of a file.)

You can't always depend on seeing a line like this in a Post-Script file, since it isn't really needed by the printer. It is just a comment that is included for our benefit. But most applications produce some sort of page count at the end.

You can control what printer a file goes to, cancel print jobs, or monitor the print queue.

Once a file has been converted to PostScript, you can't control the resulting output, but you can control what printer it goes to and how many copies are printed. You can also cancel print jobs, and monitor a job's progress on a printer queue.

There are, of course, some parts of the print process that aren't under your control as a user. An application, print command, printer daemon, or even the physical printer itself might not work as it is supposed to, over the entire computer system. If the problem is a systemwide one (other than running out of paper or toner), you'll probably need help to solve it.

However, when you have trouble printing, it's often something that you *can* solve on your own.

You can use the lpc status or lpstat –t command to identify printers.

In most UNIX environments, you have more than one printer to choose from. You might want to send a print job to a certain printer because:

- It's closest to your desk
- It's a faster printer and you have a very large job
- It doesn't have other jobs already queued to it and you're in a hurry
- It has 1200 dpi resolution and you need a high-quality printout for reproduction
- It has special fonts that you need in order to print

You can find out the names of printers by using the *lpc status* command on a BSD–based system, or the *lpstat –t* command on a System V–based system.

The *lpc status* command on a BSD–based system tells you what printers are available and whether they have any jobs on their queues (which is often all you care about, to find the printer with the shortest queue). For example:

```
% lpc status
emu:
        queuing is enabled
        printing is enabled
        2 entries in spool area
        emu is ready and printing
opal:
        queuing is enabled
        printing is enabled
        5 entries in spool area
        opal is ready and printing
rheas:
        queuing is enabled
        printing is enabled
        no entries
        no daemon present
        . . .
```

If you are looking for the shortest queue, you'll want to send your job to *rheas*. *opal* has five jobs, and *emu* has two.

(Although *rheas* says "no daemon present," this doesn't mean it isn't functioning, just that it isn't currently active.)

The *lpstat –t* command on a System V–based system shows similar information in a different form:

```
% lpstat -t
scheduler is running
system default destination: emu
system for emu: ruby.ora.com
system for opal: opal.ora.com
emu accepting requests since Wed Feb  8 15:10:18 EST 1995
opal accepting requests since Wed Feb  8 15:13:47 EST 1995
printer opal is idle. enabled since Wed Feb  8 15:10:24 EST
1995. available.
printer emu now printing emu-005. enabled since Wed Feb  8
15:13:49 EST 1995. available.
emu-005 jade.ora.com!lmui    1443    Feb 08 17:57 on emu
```

Here, the printer named *opal* has no current jobs, while a print job is currently on *emu*.

On BSD–derived UNIX, printers are defined in /etc/printcap.

The printers that are available to a BSD UNIX system are defined in the file */etc/printcap*. Among other things, */etc/printcap* tells the printer daemon how to connect to the printer, what filters to run the file through, the length and width of each page, where to send error messages, etc. It also defines *aliases* for printers, which are alternative names you can use for a printer. For example, a printer call *lp3* might be aliased to the friendlier name *sales* if it is located in the sales department.

All this is set up by your system administrator and is out of your control. What you can use */etc/printcap* for is to find out the names of the printers at your site. Even if most of the file looks like gibberish to you, look for the initial line of each entry. That line identifies the printer, each of its aliases, and what sort of printer it is:

```
emu|emu_ps|lp|ruby_ps|AppleLaserWriterIIg via EtherTalk:\
        :lp=/usr/spool/lpd/emu/emu:\
        :sd=/usr/spool/lpd/emu:pl#72:pw#85:mx#0:\
        :lf=/var/adm/lpd-errs:\
        :if=/usr/local/cap/emu:\
        :of=/usr/local/cap/papof:
```

```
opal|opal_lp|NeXT laserprinter: \
        :lp=:sd=/usr/spool/lpd/opal_lp\
        :rm=opal.ora.com:rp=opal_lp:\
        :lf=/var/adm/lpd-errs:mx#0:

linotype|Linotronic_100:\
        :lp=:sd=/usr/spool/lpd/linotype/
        :rm=ma_apple_gateway.ora.com:\
        :rp=linotype:\
        :lf=/var/adm/lpd-errs:mx#0:
```

These are entries for an Apple Laserwriter called *emu*, a NeXT laser printer called *opal,* and a Linotronic typesetter called *linotype.*

Each user is assigned a default printer.

When you send a job to print, the default printer is used unless you specify otherwise. To find out which printer is your default, try looking at the PRINTER environment variable:

```
% echo $PRINTER
opal
```

In this case, you are using the printer named *opal.*

If the PRINTER environment variable isn't set, then you're using the system default. On a BSD–based system, the default is whatever printer is named *lp*. *lp* is often "aliased" to another printer name; to find out which printer it's linked to on your site, look in the file */etc/printcap* for a line containing *lp* surrounded by vertical bars:

```
emu|emu_ps|lp|ruby_ps|AppleLaserWriterIIg via EtherTalk:\
        :lp=/usr/spool/lpd/emu/emu:\
        :sd=/usr/spool/lpd/emu:pl#72:pw#85:mx#0:\
        :lf=/var/adm/lpd-errs:\
        :if=/usr/local/cap/emu:\
        :of=/usr/local/cap/papof:
```

From the first line, you see that *lp* is aliased to the printer called *emu.*

On a System V–based system, the system default is shown when you type *lpstat –d*:

```
% lpstat -d
system default destination: emu
```

Change the printer you use on the command line or with the PRINTER environment variable.

If you want to use a different printer, there are several ways to do so. For changing the destination of a single print job, you can use a command-line option to *lp* or *lpr*. For example, if you use *lpr*, you can have the job sent to a different printer using the −*P* command-line option. To send a file called *ch00.ps* to a printer called *ibis*, type:

```
% lpr -Pibis ch00.ps
```

If you use the *lp* command, you can use the −*d* command-line option to specify a different printer. For example:

```
% lp -dibis ch00.ps
```

To change the default printer, use the PRINTER environment variable in your *.cshrc* or *.profile* file. (See Chapter 3 for more information on environment variables.) For example, to set the PRINTER variable to *ibis* in the *.cshrc* startup file, include the line:

```
setenv PRINTER ibis
```

In the *.profile* file, the syntax is different:

```
PRINTER=ibis
export PRINTER
```

You can also change the default printer for just your current terminal session (and if you're using multiple windows, for just that one window), by setting the PRINTER variable on the command line. For example, to change your default printer to *ibis* under the C shell, type:

```
% setenv PRINTER ibis
```

If you use the Bourne, Korn, or Bash shell (usually a $ prompt), type:

```
$ PRINTER=ibis
$ export PRINTER
```

All subsequent print jobs sent from that terminal session will use *ibis* as their default printer.

Check the printer queue to see the status of your print job.

Once you've sent something to the printer, you can check if it's printing by checking the printer queue. On a BSD–based system, check the queue with the *lpq* command:

```
% lpq
emu is ready and printing
Rank   Owner  Job  Files          Total Size
active bob    420  RELNOTES.ps    138331 bytes
1st    bob    421  standard input 13284 bytes
2nd    lois   422  standard input 1928 bytes
```

Bob owns the job that is currently printing, as well as the first job on the queue. Lois's job won't print until both of Bob's jobs are finished. By checking the print queue after a few minutes, Lois can wait until her job doesn't appear on the queue anymore before she makes the trek down to the printer room to pick up her document.

Like the *lpr* command, *lpq* uses your default printer (i.e., whatever printer is in your PRINTER environment variable, or *lp* if none). Also like *lpr*, you can override that value using the *–P* command-line option. For example, you can see the queue for the printer named *dodo* with the following command line:

```
% lpq –Pdodo
```

On a System V–based system, the *lpstat –t* command shows printer queues, among gobs of other information:

```
% lpstat -t
scheduler is running
system default destination: dodo
...
ibis-013 lois  1443   Feb 08 18:36 on ibis
dodo-014 peter 17493  Feb 08 18:36 on dodo
```

If the printer queue isn't moving, a large file could be processing.

Sometimes you may find that the queue doesn't seem to be moving. In that case, it might be that the printer is out of paper, the printer is jammed, or someone else is in the middle of printing a very long job.

Just because the printer queue isn't moving doesn't mean that something's wrong.

If a file is very big or if the system is very slow, then it will take a long time for the job to be sent to the printer. On the printer queue, you can see how big a print job is. A job that's 1200 bytes will print much faster than one that's a million bytes. The number of bytes doesn't necessarily correspond to the number of pages; 1,000,000 bytes might be 50 pages of text or just one page of graphics.

If you're really impatient, take a walk down to the printer room and see if the job is printing. Many printers have a light on the side that blinks to show that it's receiving input or processing; if the light is blinking, be patient; a big graphics file might take several minutes to print.

Check the obvious. The printer might be out of paper, jammed, or "hung." A red light usually comes on when the printer is out of paper or jammed.

You can cancel your print job with the lprm or cancel command.

If you have sent a job to the printer that you want to cancel, you can remove it from the print queue using either the *lprm* or *cancel* commands, depending on whether you have a System V– or BSD–derived version of UNIX.

On a BSD–derived system, use the *lprm* command with the printer job number. For example, suppose a mythical user named Lois uses the *lpq* command and discovers that she sent a job twice:

```
% lpq
emu is ready and printing
Rank    Owner  Job   Files           Total Size
active  bob    420   RELNOTES.ps     138331 bytes
1st     bob    421   standard input  13284 bytes
2nd     lois   422   standard input  1928 bytes
3rd     lois   423   standard input  1928 bytes
```

Rather than waste paper, she chooses to remove one of the identical print jobs. She uses the job number reported by *lpq* and applies that to the *lprm* command:

```
% lprm 422
dfA422ruby dequeued
```

```
cfA422ruby dequeued
```

If she had decided to delete both print jobs on her default printer, she could omit the job number:

```
% lprm
dfA422ruby dequeued
cfA422ruby dequeued
cfA423ruby dequeued
cfA423ruby dequeued
```

Without arguments, *lprm* removes all print jobs belonging to you on the target printer.

Notice that you cannot remove someone else's job. So even if Lois wanted to, there's no way for her to remove Bob's jobs and put hers at the top without the administrator's assistance.

On a System V–based system, use the *cancel* command. First use *lpstat* to find out the job number:

```
% lpstat
ibis-007 lois 1443   Feb 08 18:22 on ibis
```

Then use the job number with the *cancel* command.

```
% cancel ibis-007
request "ibis-007" cancelled
```

To cancel all your jobs, use *cancel –u* with your user name:

```
% cancel -u lois
request "ibis-8" cancelled
request "dodo-10" cancelled
```

Rebooting will fix a "hung" printer.

The printer is a piece of hardware, and like any hardware, it can get confused. For example, although most printers should be able to survive receiving non-PostScript text, some of them might have a (figurative) coughing fit and not recover until you reboot.

Rebooting the printer is usually just a matter of turning it off and on again. However, there are some printers that have more complicated procedures. If you've never rebooted your printer before, check with your system administrator that this is okay.

Since rebooting is considered a drastic measure, you should be very careful about doing it. Be sure of the following before you reboot:

- The printer is really, truly hung. Remember to be patient—a large graphic could make a page take five minutes or longer to print on a printer that doesn't have a lot of memory.

- The job that the printer is hung on is *your* job. If someone else's job is the one that the printer is having trouble with, then the courteous thing to do is just bring it to their attention.

Fonts can look wrong if the fonts requested aren't loaded on a printer.

When you send a file to a printer, the file usually requests specific fonts. Sometimes the fonts are "standard" fonts that are built into the printer, such as Courier or Times. However, some documents request special fonts that the printer may not recognize. In those cases, the printer usually has a font to use as a default font. However, the default font that it uses will not match the spacing specified in the PostScript file, so what you may see is letters scrunched up together, or letters too far apart.

What to do? Ask your administrator whether the font can be downloaded to the printer. Sometimes downloading a font is a trivial task; but be aware that in some situations, it can become a large undertaking for the administrator. If the font isn't available, then see whether you can recreate the file using different fonts.

You can find out what fonts are used by a PostScript file by looking in the file for lines with the string "DocumentFonts", and the lines immediately following them:

```
%%DocumentFonts: Symbol Times-Italic Times-Roman
%%DocumentFonts: Helvetica-Bold
%%+ Palatino-Roman
%%+ Palatino-Italic
%%+ Courier
%%+ Courier-Bold
```

Quick Reference
to printing

Information to find and keep

How do I print a text file? _____

_____

How do I print a *troff* file? *TeX* file? _____

_____

Who at this office is the best source for *troff/TeX*

questions?_____

What programs do we have for viewing, converting,

and printing graphics files? _____

_____

What printers do we have? Where are they located?

What special features do they have (color, finer reso-

lution, stationery trays, greater speed, fonts, etc.)?

_____

_____

_____

_____

How do I change a toner cartridge? (Where do I find

the cartridges; which cartridges do I use for which

printers; where do I put the used cartridges for recy-

cling, etc.?) _____

_____

_____

_____

How do I reboot the printer(s), or should I never do

this? _____

_____

Who do I contact about printer problems? _____

_____

If something is wrong with the printer hardware, what

phone number should be called for service? Who at

our site is authorized to request service? _____

_____

What is my default printer?_____

_____

To print a PostScript file

To print a file called *memo.ps* on a BSD–based system:

    % lpr memo.ps

To print a file called *memo.ps* on a System V–based
system:

    % lp memo.ps

Problems printing PostScript

1. Look for error messages.
2. Check that the output file is a PostScript file. (If you
   print directly from an application, print to a Post-
   Script file instead of sending the output to a
   printer.) The first line of the file should start with
   the characters:

       %!

   If it doesn't, the file isn't PostScript.
3. Ask if other people are having trouble printing to
   the same printer.
4. Try printing a short PostScript file that you have
   successfully printed in the past.

5. Reboot the printer and try again, sending a short PostScript file that has printed in the past. If this doesn't work, something could be wrong with the printer, printer daemon, or network. Ask your system administrator for help.

   If the old PostScript file does print, then you know that the problem is with your application or source file.

Check available printers, default printer

1. Identify printers, with either

   % lpc status

   or

   % lpstat -t

2. Check your default printer

   % echo $PRINTER

Change the default printer

1. To make a permanent change, edit your setup file. (This varies by your environment.) For example, to change your default printer in the *.cshrc* file to ibis:

   setenv PRINTER ibis

   To change your default printer in the *.profile* file to ibis:

   PRINTER=ibis
   export PRINTER

   To change the printer for a single print command, use the *lpr–P* or *lp–d*. For example, to print the file *memo.ps* to the printer ibis:

   % lpr -Pibis memo.ps

   or

   % lp -dibis memo.ps

My file isn't printing

1. Check the default printer queue. On BSD:

   % lpq

   If you need to check the queue of another printer, name the printer:

   % lpq -Pibis

   To check the queue on System V:

   % lpstat -t

You will see if there are jobs ahead of you, how large the jobs are, if the printer thinks that a job is active, and—with some printers—whether the printer is out of paper.

2. Be patient. Large jobs can take a long time to process.

3. If the queue has jobs on it, but the jobs don't seem to be advancing, check the obvious: is the printer printing pages, is the green light blinking, is the printer out of paper or jammed?

Cancel a job in the print queue

List the jobs in queue, to see the number.

   % lpq

or

   % lpstat

Cancel the job with lprm or cancel; e.g, to cancel job number 432 on BSD:

   % lprm 432

To cancel job ibis-344 on System V:

   % cancel ibis-344

To cancel all your jobs that are queued, type:

   % lprm

or

   % cancel -u yourname

What you need to know about printing

CHAPTER 6

What you need to know about space and time

You share space and time with other users.

UNIX is a multiuser system. This means just what it sounds like: many different users might be working on the same UNIX computer at the same time.

When you live alone, you can leave dishes in the sink, play the stereo all night, and take as long as you want in the shower. When you compute on a standalone system (like a single-user PC at home), you can leave applications running or have a Star Trek sound file play each time you log on. In both cases, the only person who will mind is you. If you have to wait to start the word processor because the Star Trek theme is playing, that's fine: you've set your own priorities.

When you live with roommates in the same house, you need to be more aware of others. No one probably cares if you have a mess in your own closet, but if you routinely clutter up common areas, you'll probably irritate others.

When you compute with others on the same system, you also have to be more aware. You could think of your UNIX system as a space that you share with all your coworkers. Instead of sharing a living room, bathroom, and kitchen, you're sharing disk space, system memory, and processing time.

Sharing with others

Most of the time, I'm not even aware I'm sharing the system with others, except when it gets slow or I need to share files with someone else.

Carol Vogt

Even if your system resources are adequate today, they may not be tomorrow.

If your system is operating close to capacity, you might be painfully aware of system resources. You might have to wait for programs to respond, take your place in long print queues, routinely clean out your home directory to conserve space, turn off fancy screen savers, or eschew reading certain newsgroups that your system no longer has the room to store.

If you have a smoothly running system with adequate resources—or if you work alone at night after everyone else has gone home—you might not even notice that you're on a multiuser system. Response time to your commands might be nearly instantaneous, and you might not be aware of any upper limits on storage space. But don't get smug about it, your time will come.

No matter how smoothly your system runs today, demands on most systems are increasing. New people get hired. Environments include more capabilities and user options. Programs and applications are updated to new versions that are smarter, more graphical, and more resource-intensive. More information is stored online. Computers are networked to remote machines.

Ten years ago, a standard company environment might have been a Wyse terminal with a single character display, running on a computer with a serial connection. Now, a standard environment in that same company might be a color X terminal with graphic applications like Mosaic and FrameMaker, running on a computer with full Internet access. Each of those "improvements" requires more system resources.

We continue to ask more of our computer systems, and we continue to run up against limits, of both disk space and system time. Chances are, at some time you'll be asked to conserve disk space by removing extraneous files or to use less system time by stopping unnecessary processes.

Files are stored on disks.

On any computer system, files are saved on a disks. There are two kinds of disks: floppy disks (which are small, portable, and easily exchanged), and hard disks (which are larger and not as easily detached from the computer).

On a standalone PC or Macintosh, you can visualize disks easily. On DOS, your prompt tells you what disk you're currently in (e.g., C:\>); on a Macintosh, you see each disk as a separate icon at the right edge of your desktop. On a PC or Macintosh, you are always aware of what disk you're currently working in. UNIX, on the other hand, tries to make the distinction between hard disks seamless. So on UNIX, it's sometimes a little harder to keep track of what disk you're currently working in.

Without the computer, a hard disk is just a big hunk of metal. It needs to be made accessible to the computer's operating system before it can be used for storing files. When a hard disk is made accessible on the computer, we say that the disk is "mounted." All this means is that you can now read and write files from that big hunk of metal via the magic of the operating system.

On UNIX, disks are mounted as directories, or filesystems.

On UNIX, we tend to think of files as residing in directories, and we think of those directories as branches of a single system directory tree. What UNIX keeps hidden from users is that the directory tree is composed of several different hard disks, which are just patched together by the operating system to look like a cohesive whole.

For example, you may be used to having files in your home directory, and also in another directory (for example, /projects). Files in /home might be stored on a different hard disk than files in /projects, but since you can move between the two directories easily, and move or copy files between them easily, you don't think about them as being on separate disks.

In UNIX jargon, each of the directory trees corresponding to a different disk is called a *filesystem*. So you would say that moving a file from the /home filesystem to the /projects filesystem moves the file from one disk to another. (Technically, the one-to-one correspondence described here is a little simplistic: some sites might be set up with more than one filesystem on a

Floppy disks aren't usually used on UNIX systems

Although some UNIX systems have floppy disk drives, floppies are seldom used in UNIX. The primary use for floppies has been for transferring files, and on UNIX systems there are usually much more efficient ways to transfer files than putting them on a physical disk.

single disk, or with a filesystem distributed across several different disks for maximum performance.)

There are likely to be several different hard disks mounted on your system. These disks are usually divided by function. For example, /home is a filesystem that is frequently used for users' home directories. On our system, we use a filesystem called /work for book production, and we keep USENET news on another filesystem mounted as /var/spool/news. It's done this way because it's easier to maintain, and also because it means that if news fills up with thousands of articles about the new Star Trek series, our book production group doesn't have to suffer for it.

Note that the mounted directories can be staggered: that is, we mount /usr/local as a separate filesystem under /usr. So not all filesystems have to be mounted at the root level.

Disk space is shared on UNIX systems.

UNIX users usually don't see the physical disks, nor are users typically aware of how much disk space might be available, until they get a message from their system administrator saying that disk space is low.

On UNIX, disk space is shared among all the users on the system. So if someone else puts a giant file in their home directory, it may affect the amount of space left in your home directory. When disks are nearly full, files need to be removed, compressed, archived, or moved to another disk.

If one disk becomes filled up, there may still be room on another disk. When you get a message that /home is filled up, you might be able to move files from /home to another filesystem (for example, /projects) and that will help open up space on /home. But it's better to just tell your system administrator, since moving files around just to clear up disk space isn't the best policy.

Some filesystems are mounted from remote machines.

Most UNIX systems today support some sort of remote file sharing. The most common of these is the Network File System, or NFS.

What you need to know about space and time

Under NFS, you can mount a directory from another machine as a filesystem. This means that the actual files reside on a disk elsewhere on the network—perhaps on Norm's machine down the hall or on Eric's machine on the other side of the country.

At our company, we have two main offices, one in California and one in Massachusetts. When users from California come here, they find all the files that they use every day, remotely mounted onto our machine. The files are still being read and written on the hard disk in California, but users can work on them here in Massachusetts—it just takes a little bit longer to open and write files and to list directories.

You can look at disk names and the space available on each disk.

Take a look at the disk space available on your system. The *df* command tells you what filesystems there are on the system and how much space is currently available for them.

The output of *df* depends on what type of UNIX system you use. On a BSD system, you see something like the following:

```
% df
Filesystem        kbytes  used    avail   capacity  Mounted on
/dev/dsk/c0t3d0s0 89383   76272   4181    95%       /
/dev/dsk/c0t3d0s3 217671  168675  27236   86%       /usr
/dev/dsk/c0t3d0s5 497478  202322  245416  45%       /usr/local
/dev/dsk/c0t3d0s4 96455   40011   46804   46%       /home
```

In this listing, each filesystem is listed on a separate line. For each filesystem, the listing shows:

- The name of the device associated with the filesystem. For example, for /*home*, the device is /*dev/dsk/c0t3d0s4*. (In general, you should never have to concern yourself with this.)

- The total amount of space on the disk. For example, the /*home* filesystem has a total of 96,455 kilobytes.

- The amount of space that is currently used. For example, on /*home*, 40,011 kilobytes of the disk are being used.

- The amount of space that is still free. On /*home*, 46,804 kilobytes are free.

- The percentage of the filesystem that is currently filled

- The name of the filesystem

Some systems have automatic deletions

We have a great system. Our administrator created a cron script that deletes any file that starts with a comma after a few days. I always use this convention when creating any kind of temporary file. I name a file something like ,letter and a few days later it's automatically deleted without me having to remember. That's like being able to litter in your own home and not worry about picking up after yourself. (Now if I could only get it to work at home...)

Mike Sierra

Disk space is represented by the BSD *df* command as the number of kilobytes. Each kilobyte is 1,024 bytes. For example, notice that the */usr* filesystem is at 86% capacity, with 27,236 kilobytes left, or about 27 megabytes. This sounds like a lot, but someone transferring one big file could finish it off.

On a System V–based system, the output of *df* is different. Instead of giving information in terms of kilobytes and percentages, System V *df* gives the number of blocks and files that are used:

```
% df
/            (/dev/dsk/c0t3d0s0 ):   26222 blocks    42033 files
/usr         (/dev/dsk/c0t3d0s3 ):   97992 blocks    95767 files
/usr/local(/dev/dsk/c0t3d0s5 ):     590312 blocks   238817 files
/home        (/dev/dsk/c0t3d0s4 ):  112888 blocks    47710 files
```

It's harder to translate this into useful information for users, since you have to know how big a block is on each disk before you can know how much space is actually being used. Luckily, many System V–based machines also support a *–k* command-line option for a BSD–compatible *df* display:

```
% df -k
Filesystem          kbytes   used    avail   capacity  Mounted on
/dev/dsk/c0t3d0s0 89383    76272   4181    95%       /
/dev/dsk/c0t3d0s3 217671   168675  27236   86%       /usr
/dev/dsk/c0t3d0s5 497478   202322  245416  45%       /usr/local
/dev/dsk/c0t3d0s4 96455    40011   46804   46%       /home
```

You can look at how much disk space your files take up.

How do you find out how much space you're using up? Most users don't think in terms of disk space, but in terms of files and directories. You know some files are bigger than others, but it's hard to get perspective on how big a drop they are in the ocean of disk space.

To be a good citizen, you should start paying attention to how much disk space you use up. As most users already know, you can find out how big files are by running *ls –l*:

```
% ls -l
total 139
-rw-r----- 1 lmui 2769     Mar 31 11:54  author_copy
-rw-r--r-- 1 lmui 2163514 Sep 16 1993    ch07.ps
-rw------- 1 lmui 18216   Sep 19 13:22   dead.letter
-rw-rw---- 1 lmui 20181   May 13 12:14   mbox
```

```
-rw-r----- 1 lmui 743      Aug 30 09:58  people
-rw------- 1 lmui 13378    Jun 16 14:29  tmpmail
```

The size of the file is shown in number of characters (or bytes).

You don't have to understand anything about bytes or kilobytes or megabytes to do rough comparisons. The file *ch07*.ps in this directory is the largest by far. It's 2,163,514 bytes (~2,000 kilobytes or 2 megabytes). That's over 99% of the space taken up by this directory and almost 1,000 times larger than the text file called *author_copy*.

You can look at the size of your directories and subdirectories.

In addition to using *ls –l* to find out how big a particular file is, you can find out how much space an entire directory is using up with the du command. For example:

```
% du
563    ./misc
2      ./Mail/inbox
1      ./Mail/drafts
1      ./Mail/detach.dir
1      ./Mail/index.dir
2573   ./Mail/SAVED
564    ./Mail/94.03.08
482    ./Mail/94.01.03
232    ./Mail/INACTIVE
7185   ./Mail
92     ./mgmt/coop
99     ./mgmt
   ...
```

By default, *du* shows you the size of each subdirectory before it shows you the total size of the directory. This is useful if you want to track down where all your disk space is. For example, this listing tells me that most of my space is taken up saving mail messages. But if you want to know a total for a directory, it's better to use the *–s* option to get just a grand total:

```
% du -s
14942 .
```

du reports sizes in kilobytes, which is the same unit used by *df*. If you remove a large file, you'll see the difference when you next run *du*. For example, if I remove a 2,000-kilobyte file, that change is reflected in my *du* listing:

You don't have to know a kilobyte from a megabyte to do some rough comparisons

A twenty-line ASCII mail message is somewhere around 500 bytes, or 1/2000th of a megabyte.

A 300-page book might be 1 megabyte in ASCII form, 1 megabyte in *troff* form, 3 megabytes in FrameMaker, and 20 megabytes in PostScript.

A scanned-in GIF picture of your favorite television personality might be 50,000 bytes, or 1/20 of a megabyte. The PostScript version of the same picture might be half a megabyte. A picture scanned in at higher resolution will be much larger.

A 1–minute sound clip of your favorite band might be half a megabyte.

```
% ls -l ch07.ps
-rw-r--r-- 1 lmui 2163514 Sep 16 1993 ch07.ps
% rm ch07.ps
% du -s
12814   .
```

If I typed *df* now too, I might see that an extra 2,000 kilobytes are free for the filesystem */home* as a whole, as well. (Or I might not see any change, since other people are removing and creating files simultaneously. For example, someone else might have just added a large file to the system at the same time I removed one. But don't worry, it did make a difference.)

You can check the disk space available on the filesystem that the current directory resides on by giving . (the current directory) as an argument to *df*. For example:

```
% df .
Filesystem   kbytes   used     avail   capacity  Mounted on
/dev/sd1g    1308070  1236571  58419   95%       /home
```

Commands may create temporary files that also take up disk space.

The actual files that you're creating aren't the only users of disk space. When you run a command, the command often creates temporary files. Usually, these files are hidden from you and should stay that way. But you should know about temporary files so you have a better idea of the impact of your actions on the system.

For example, right now I'm editing this chapter using *vi*. When I'm editing a file, *vi* creates temporary buffers in another directory. On our system, these buffers are kept in */tmp*. So right now, when I look in */tmp*, I see two files belonging to me:

```
% ls -l /tmp | egrep lmui
    ...
-rw------- 1 lmui 13312 Sep 26 11:19 Ex23008
-rw------- 1 lmui 10240 Sep 26 11:17 Rx23008
    ...
```

Obviously, the bigger the file you're editing, the bigger the temporary file. When you exit *vi*, these files are removed.

Other programs also create temporary files. For example, mailer programs often make a copy of your mail file, either in your home directory or in a systemwide temporary directory. FrameMaker creates several temporary files, mostly backup files and a lock file, all in the current directory. The Emacs editor creates backup files with trailing tildes (~). When using a network retrieval program like Mosaic, files are copied into /*tmp*.

Usually, these files are deleted when the program exits. However, if the program is suddenly interrupted or killed, these files aren't always removed. And sometimes they aren't removed at all. For example, both Emacs and FrameMaker are designed to retain the backup files.

Clean up your directories occasionally (or when you get a warning).

If you get a message from your system administrator to clean out your home directory, how do you think about what to erase?

First of all, look for the big space hogs that make the most difference. Do you really still need that PostScript file? Do you need to keep that GIF file of Calvin and Hobbes? Do you still need all seven parts to the *rec.pets.dogs* FAQ list?

Then there are the little files. No, they don't take up a lot of space, but removing (or combining) them will make it easier to find things in your directory. Do you need to hold onto that to-do list from last April? Do you need to keep that copy of a pumpkin pie recipe that didn't come out that well? Do you still want that advertisement from someone selling a washing machine that you took off the *ne.forsale* newsgroup last month?

Look for files that are clearly temporary files. In fact, you might use a few naming conventions to make it easier for you to find files that you can remove. For example, I always name files *tmp* or *foo* when I know I won't need them for more than a few minutes.

Some sites deal with disk space issues by enforcing *disk quotas* on their users. If your site uses disk quotas, then you are restricted to a specified amount of disk space on your home directory. You can see how much space you have allotted (and how much you've used up) using the *quota* command. Under disk quotas, conserving disk space isn't a matter of being a good citizen, it's a way of life.

Removing files safely

Files are removed under UNIX using the *rm* command. Unlike other operating systems, there's nothing like Norton Utilities for UNIX. Once a file is gone, it's gone. Often you can find it on a backup tape, but you can't recover it from the disk. So you have to be particularly careful with the *rm* command.

One way to be careful is to use your shell's aliasing feature to alias *rm* to /*bin*/*rm* –*i*. With the –*i* option, you are prompted before any files are actually removed:

```
% rm -i core
rm: remove core? y
```

The file is not removed unless you type y and press the Return key.

To install this alias, enter the following line into your *.cshrc* or *.tcshrc* file:

```
alias rm /bin/rm -i
```

Or enter the following line into your *.profile* or *.bashrc* file:

```
alias rm='/bin/rm -i'
```

Now whenever you use *rm*, you are prompted:

```
% rm core
rm: remove core? y
```

Don't forget to check saved mail messages.

Mail messages are a controversial topic. Everyone has their own way of maintaining mail messages, and it's partly a matter of preference and partly habit.

Some people keep mail messages in appropriate directories. For example, if you have a directory containing contracts for the Acme company, you might save all mail from that company in that directory.

Other people just keep mail messages in separate files in their home directory (or a subdirectory thereof). So you'll have a home directory with files called *lost.coat*, *newproject*, *adrians.address*, etc.

Some people create files for each discrete topic. So all messages about the Christmas party go into a file called *party*, all messages about the 401k plan go into a file called *401k*, etc.

Some of us keep messages in files named after who sent the message (my own preference). So all messages from Tim are kept in a file called *tim*.

And other people just keep all messages, regardless of the topic or sender, in the *mbox* file in their home directory.

Sometimes when you're cleaning your home directory, you might take the time to go through your mail folders and remove the messages you don't need anymore. But even if you don't, you can still make a difference by removing the big messages. For example, if Steve sent you a *tar* archive in email, you've probably already untarred it, and you don't need to keep it in your mail archives. If you save your own messages (which I do; shh, don't tell anyone), you can weed out the messages you were only forwarding to others, you can remove the 20-page PostScript file you mailed out to your editor, and you can remove the messages reminding your brother about your mother's birthday.

Always remove a "core" file.

Sometimes you may see a giant unreadable file called *core* in your directory.

This file is usually created because a program crashed and burned. As a general rule, good programs should never produce core files—but many do. Programmers can often debug a program by examining the core file, but for users, a core file is just a big file with no redeeming value. Use the *file* command to confirm that it's a core file:

```
% file core
core:core file
```

and if it is a core file, remove it:

```
% rm core
```

On many systems, core files are automatically removed when they are several days old. So don't be surprised if your core file disappears on its own (but don't count on it!) Also, don't create files on UNIX called *core*, since they might just disappear on you.

Some UNIX shells allow you to limit the size of the core dumps you create. So one way you might avoid creating large core files is to limit the size of core files to 0. If you use the C shell or *tcsh*, you might type:

```
% limit coredumpsize 0
```

If you use *ksh* or *bash*, type:

```
% ulimit -c 0
```

Look for temporary files that weren't removed after they were created.

Sometimes, temporary files are kept in the directory you're working in. For example, Emacs saves buffers to filenames with a tilde (~) suffix. Each file you edit has its own tilde file, so you'll see both *chapter1* and *chapter1~* in a directory. These files are not removed when you quit Emacs. FrameMaker creates *.backup* files that aren't removed when you quit out of the program.

If you and other users in your company frequently use an application that creates large temporary files, then you might talk to your system administrator about having them automatically removed on a periodic basis. For example, our system administrator has set it up so that FrameMaker *.backup* files are automatically removed when they are three days old.

Home is full

As an administrator, I have to keep an eye on disk space and make sure that we have enough resources to keep working.

Periodically, I send out mail to everyone saying that /home is 100% full and people should clean out their home directories. Things usually clear up, but I know that it's just a few users who are making the difference. Most users have no idea what I'm talking about.

Tanya Herlick
administrator

I never think about disk space. The disk is the *magic* part. When Tanya says /home is full, I delete some things, but I don't know whether it's helping or whether it matters, and I don't have much to delete anyway.

Jane Appleyard

Remove files that you can easily recreate as needed.

When space gets tight, I also remove files that I know I can reproduce or retrieve again easily. For example, I have a directory of FAQ lists from USENET newsgroups. When space gets tight, I just remove them all—they are reposted once a month anyway, and if I can't wait that long I can always find them on an FTP site.

Or I might have a figure in both GIF and PostScript formats, and I'll remove the PostScript version since I know I can always recreate it from the GIF file.

Some of the biggest files on any system are PostScript files that were saved for printing via *lpr* or for sending a manuscript over email or floppy. PostScript files can often be recreated as needed, so why keep them around? You should make a habit of removing or compressing PostScript files once you don't need them any more.

If you save files, you can compress them to take up less room.

If you want to save a file, but won't be using it very often, then you can *compress* it to make it take up less space. For example, let's suppose I have a PostScript file that I want to hold on to for sentimental reasons:

```
% ls -l kitty.ps
-rw-r-----  1 lmui 1593548 Oct 18 16:56 kitty.ps
```

This is a big file, and my administrator could rightfully be annoyed that I want to keep it around. However, I can ease my conscience a little by compressing it with the *compress* command:

```
% compress kitty.ps
```

The file is compressed and given a *.Z* extension. If I list the compressed file, I see that it's now much smaller:

```
% ls -l kitty.ps.Z
-rw-r-----  1 lmui 45182 Oct 18 16:56 kitty.ps.Z
```

The file is now more than 35 times smaller! As it turns out, some file formats compress more tightly than others, and PostScript files compress particularly well.

What you need to know about space and time

In the compressed format, the file cannot be used as easily. For example, you cannot send this compressed PostScript file directly to the printer. However, whenever you want the file back in its full, uncompressed glory, just use the *uncompress* command:

```
% uncompress kitty.ps
```

(The *.Z* suffix is optional to *uncompress*.)

Here's a nice tip: if all you want to do is print the compressed PostScript file, then you can save yourself some steps using the *zcat* command. *zcat* doesn't actually create an uncompressed file, but just outputs it to your terminal. If you pipe the *zcat* output directly to *lpr*, you save yourself the steps of having to run *lpr* separately and compressing the file again once you're done.

```
% zcat kitty.ps | lpr
```

You can do something similar whenever you want to use a compressed file as input to another command.

compress is the most common compression command on UNIX systems, but it isn't the only one by far. Other methods are *gzip* and *zip*.

If you have a whole directory of files that you don't need immediate access to anymore, you can compress them all at once:

```
% compress *
```

When you get a message that a disk is full, first find out which filesystem is affected.

When a filesystem is full, you find out the hard way. For me, it always happens when I'm editing a file in *vi*. I try writing the file and I get the message:

```
Write failed, filesystem is full!
```

Or I'm just typing away, and suddenly I get placed in the colon prompt with the message:

```
No space left on device
```

These two messages may sound like the same thing, but they signify space problems in different parts of the filesystem.

Home is full

I sometimes create a directory for some fleeting reason, inside which I place several megabytes of something, and then promptly forget about it for a couple of months. When home is full, I need to look at all my subdirectories. (I use a command called vtree, or you can use du.) Otherwise, it would probably never occur to me that at one time I placed a zillion graphic files in some deeply nested directory called "graphics."

Anything that I really need but am not using very much, I can compress with gzip. Text files compress by about 50%, and many graphic files compress down to nearly nothing.

Mike Sierra

When you get an error message (*Write failed, filesystem is full!*) trying to write a file, it means that the filesystem in which the file resides is out of space. For example, if you're trying to write the file to */work/sysbook/ch01*, it means that the filesystem */work* or */work/sysbook* is full.

When this happens, how can you save your work? Well, one way is to try to clear up some space on */work*—for example, if you know you have a big PostScript file there that you don't need any longer, you can delete it. Once you clear up some space, write the file immediately.

Another way to save your work is to write it to another filesystem. You'll probably want to move it back once space frees up again, but at least you know that you haven't lost an hour of editing. For example, if you know that the */home* filesystem is separate from */work*, you can just save the file under the */work* filesystem. Again, assuming you use *vi*, you would type:

```
:w /home/ch01.save
```

When you get the *No space left on device* message while trying to edit the file itself, then it's a more serious problem. Remember that *vi* keeps temporary files in */tmp*. The message means that */tmp* is out of space. Although you can probably write the file, beware that you probably don't want to—your buffers in */tmp* might be corrupted. You shouldn't write the file until you clear up space in */tmp* and restore your buffers.

Look in */tmp* to see if there are any files there that belong to you. For example, I know that my mailer keeps mail folders in */tmp* and that after a system crash they aren't cleaned up—so if any of those files belong to me, I remove them and then try to get *vi* working again long enough to write my file and get the heck out of there. However, often you just have to wait for the system administrator to clear up space for you.

You can follow a similar strategy when working in programs other than *vi*. If you keep track of where you're working and where your programs keep temporary files, then you have a better chance of saving work when your system runs low on disk space.

What you need to know about space and time

You may be able to retrieve deleted files from backups.

One of the most important responsibilities of a system administrator is to maintain *backups*. A backup is a periodic "snapshot" of files that is stored on a magnetic tape. The files are copied onto the tape, and can be retrieved from the tape at a later date.

Every site has its own backup policy. But since backing up a system can take a long time and can tax the system, they usually aren't done more often than once a day. Generally, backups are performed overnight, when few users might be affected.

The value of daily backups is that they can prevent catastrophes when someone accidently removes a file. As long as the file existed yesterday, then it can be recovered from the overnight backup. You won't recover any changes made to the file this morning, but at least you haven't lost a week's work.

Daily backup tapes are usually overwritten after a while. At our office, they are recycled every four weeks. However, most administrators set aside a permanent "full" backup tape on a regular basis—for example, every month. This is for situations when you don't realize until two months later that you removed a file you still need. By finding the latest backup from before you removed the file, you might be able to recover at least some version of it.

To retrieve a file off a backup tape, you need to ask your system administrator. Send the administrator email with the full pathname of the file, and the approximate date you want it from. (For example, if you know you removed a file sometime in early August, you might say "take it off the latest backup you have in July.")

UNIX systems multitask by working on each process a little at a time.

You may have heard it said that UNIX has built-in *multitasking*. This means that UNIX computers can work on more than one process simultaneously. You don't have to wait for one program to complete its business before you can start another one.

What do you do when the system is slow?

If the system is a little slow, I just suffer through it. If the system gets real slow, I bail out and start doing some other work. I check back later to see if the system is back up to speed.

Carol Vogt

A PC or Macintosh computer today can also run several programs alongside one another, but it requires applications to be "good citizens" and permit other programs to have a share of the processing pie. UNIX does it all at the operating system level. This doesn't mean much to users any more, but it's important to programmers and computer scientists.

A single-processor UNIX system actually does work on only one process at a time, but it works in very small time slices. It gives a slice of time to each process, and then moves to the next one. If you give a command, and there are ten processes running, UNIX will give a little time to your command, a little to the second process, a little to the third, until it comes around to your command again and does a little more work on yours. UNIX works very quickly between tasks, so if the load of processes is normal, it will seem as if the computer is dedicated to fulfilling your commands.

However, systems can be slow when there are too many processes. Then it becomes painfully obvious that you are in a multiuser environment. You issue a simple command like *date* and there's a definite pause before you see any output. Or, a print command that normally takes a minute might take ten minutes or more to complete. If you use an X terminal, you may notice that your windows aren't redrawing very quickly when you move them around.

A slowdown of the system can result from a large number of people each doing a few things, or a smaller number of people doing many things.

When the system gets slow, take an inventory of what you're doing.

You know it when the system gets slow. You try to move a window, and it takes a few extra microseconds to respond. You type on the keyboard, and you have to wait for the computer to catch up with you. You print a one-page file, and it takes five minutes to get to the printer queue. A slow system is like driving in downtown traffic at 5 PM on a Friday. You wonder if you wouldn't be better off if you just pulled over and read a book until the traffic lets up.

A difference is that in a traffic jam, you're only one car. On a UNIX system, one user can be responsible for several cars, a broken stoplight, and a jack-knifed tractor-trailer by the entrance to the Interstate. So when the system gets slow, the first thing you should be doing is seeing how big a part of the problem *you* are.

You can use the ps command to see what processes you're running.

If you're not sure what processes you're running, use the *ps* command to see what you're up to:

```
% ps
PID TT STAT  TIME COMMAND
15047 r5 S    0:00 -csh (tcsh)
15052 r5 S    0:00 xcalc
 7648 s6 S    0:00 -csh (tcsh)
15058 s6 R    0:00 ps
```

This tells me that I'm running two shell programs and one *xcalc* window. *ps* also tells me that I'm running *ps*.

The caveat is that *ps* doesn't know about *everything* you're doing. For example, right now the most resource-intensive program I'm running is FrameMaker, but *ps* didn't tell me about it. It also didn't mention the *xbiff* program I'm running. The reason is that I exited the *xterm* window I started these programs in, and *ps* usually only displays processes associated with a terminal.

ps is very system-specific. The options on your system may vary, but on my system, I can use the *–x* command-line option to find all processes on the system that belong to me:

```
% ps -x
PID TT STAT  TIME COMMAND
 3323 ?  S    0:17 xlbiff
 7628 ?  I    0:00 in.rshd
 7629 ?  I    0:00 tcsh -c xterm -display opal:0
14869 ?  S    0:10 /usr/local/frame/bin/sunxm.os.sparc/maker
14875 ?  I    0:00 /usr/local/frame/bin/sunxm.os.sparc/
fm_misd -r 8 -w 11 -v 0
14878 ?  I    0:00 /usr/local/frame/bin/sunxm.os.sparc/
fm_flb
15039 ?  I    0:00 in.rshd
15040 ?  I    0:00 tcsh -c xterm -display opal:0
15047 r5 I    0:00 -csh (tcsh)
15052 r5 I    0:00 xcalc
 7648 s6 S    0:00 -csh (tcsh)
15071 s6 R    0:00 ps -x
```

What do you do when the system is slow?

I close up any extra windows I'm not using.

Cathy Record

On a UNIX machine, you can run many programs simultaneously.

When you type commands on a UNIX system, you use a UNIX shell. The shell is a program for spawning new commands. Usually, the shell waits for one command to finish before it starts a new one. For example, if you type the *cd* command and then the *ls* command, the shell waits for the *cd* command to complete before it lists the new directory. When you start a mail program on the command line, the shell waits for you to exit the mailer before it gives you another prompt.

However, when running programs that might take a long time and that aren't interactive (that is, that don't prompt you for more input in the terminal window) you may put those commands *in the background.* To put a command in the background, you simply place an ampersand at the end of the command line, like this:

```
% grep waldo * > grep.waldo &
```

This command searches through each line of each file in the directory for the text string "waldo" and prints any matching lines into the file *grep.waldo.* Since the *grep* command may take a long time to search through all the files in the directory, we put the command in the background so we don't have to wait for it to finish before we can run other commands in that shell.

When the background process ends, you'll get a message to your terminal the next time you press Return:

```
[1] Done grep waldo * > grep.waldo
```

Now for a word of caution. If you want to *grep* for many different things in a directory, you may be tempted to start several such *grep* commands one after another. For example:

```
% grep waldo * > grep.waldo &
% grep spock * > grep.spock &
% grep "holy grail" * > grep.grail &
```

This isn't always the best idea in the world, however. One of these processes won't make a big difference on the system load, but several running simultaneously might start to be noticeable. Instead, be considerate of your coworkers and don't run too many resource-intensive programs at the same time if you don't have to.

What you need to know about space and time

X users commonly have many programs running at once.

If you use the X window system, then you may have several shell windows open at the same time. You may have a graphical mailer running. You may have a calculator window open, a calendar application, and maybe something cute like a cat running across your screen. You don't need all of these programs running all the time, but X is set up so that you can have them running all the time for your convenience.

Computers were meant to be used. There's no point to having X if you're not going to run multiple windows. But when things get slow, be aware that you're part of the problem. So when the system gets slow, quit out of the calculator, exit some of those extra xterm windows, and consider whether some of the programs you're running continuously (like mailers) could be exited and just restarted as needed.

Some programs are more resource intensive than others.

Some programs make the computer work harder than others. For example, if you run the *clear* command, it just clears your screen. It doesn't need to open any files, start any subprocesses, or communicate with other programs. All it does is send a control sequence to your terminal and then bail out.

On the other hand, if you start up a mail program, the program usually opens your mail configuration file (e.g., *.mailrc*), opens your system folder, searches through it for the most recent messages, displays their headers on your screen, and then awaits your commands. In addition, many mailers copy the mail folder to another file so that the mail folder itself isn't changed until you explicitly update it or quit from the program. The mail program is clearly a more resource-intensive program than *clear*.

(Have you noticed that when you have many mail messages in your system folder, or when one of those messages is very big, the mailer takes longer to start up? This is because the program needs more time to read and copy the mail file.)

What do you do when the system is slow?

I close up any graphical applications, like my mailer, Mosaic, xrn, and use command-line programs instead.

I also make sure I don't have any memory-eating programs running, like xearth.

Stephanie Davis

What do you do when the system is slow?

I often get impatient at first. But if it gets really slow, I shut down unnecessary processes, and think of phone calls I need to make or take a few minutes to relax.

Linda Lamb

Commands with dynamic displays eat up more time than "snapshot" displays.

Some programs are designed to keep updating themselves. What's ironic is that many of these programs are used to monitor system resources, while they themselves use up more than their fair share.

A classic example is the *xload* program, which shows you the system load average in a small X window. *xload* polls the operating system every 10 seconds for the system load average, and then updates the display. While this is an appropriate tool for the person responsible for maintaining the system, so he or she will know when the system is becoming overloaded, it's unnecessary for regular users. The only reason a regular user might want to know the load average is if he or she wants to know if this is a good time to start a resource-intensive job. If that's the case, the *uptime* command will tell you the load average, and it won't add significantly to that average.

Another example is the *top* program, which is installed on many systems. *top* shows you what processes have been using up the most process time. However, you'll find that *top* itself is almost always at the top of the list, because it updates the listing every five seconds.

Even clock programs might come into play here. If you run a program that updates the time every second, then it's going to work 60 times as hard as one that updates every minute.

X programs are much more resource intensive than character-based programs.

X programs need to do more work than most character-based programs. This is because X programs are graphical. While character-based programs are limited to telling the terminal what characters to display where, X programs might tell the terminal to draw a picture of a paint brush in the upper-right corner, a little arrow icon beneath it in a shadowed box, etc. Even a character isn't just a character: X programs have many

What you need to know about space and time

different fonts available to them, which can be displayed at different sizes.

Also, since windows can be moved easily, or can be obscured by other windows and then uncovered again, X programs have to redraw their windows all the time. When you move even one window in X, several programs have to do work:

- The program that lets you move windows and keeps track of where your windows are (your *window manager*) needs to know that you're moving a window.

- The window manager tells the program that controls the window that's being moved that it needs to redraw.

- The window manager tells any programs controlling windows that were obscured by the first window that they need to redraw those portions that are now visible.

For example, suppose you have a calculator window hiding behind several *xterm* windows. Regardless of whether you've used that *xcalc* window all day, it still needs to do work whenever the window or even a portion of the window is uncovered, just to redraw the portion that's now visible.

All this is much more noticeable if you run X programs over a slow network. You'll notice that when you start a new X program, it'll take a few extra seconds before you see anything. Then you may see the window decoration appear, but the window itself will be blank. Slowly you'll see lines appear, graphics, and finally you'll get some text. All this time, you might see a small LED on your keyboard blinking away madly. That LED indicates network traffic, which usually goes so quickly that you don't notice, but on a slow network you'll get an idea of how much trouble you're really causing every time you do something simple in X.

This isn't to say that you should avoid running X programs. But when the system is slow, consider whether you still need all the programs you have running, and consider whether you can do the same work using a non-graphical application. For example, when the system gets slow, the first thing I do is exit my graphical mailer and start using a command-line mailer again (such as *mail, mush,* or *elm*).

What do you do when the system is slow?

I don't do anything. I just wait for it to get faster again. Usually it happens when there are other things I can be doing, like copy-editing on paper.

Ellen Siever

The time program
reports how much time a
command took to run. To
find out how much time a
program uses, just
precede it on the
command line with the
"time" command.

```
% time format -Tps -o3
...
4.8 real 0.5 user 0.7 sys
```

After the program has
finished running, the time
program displays the
amount of time it used,
breaking it down the time
into several components:
real time, user time, and
system time. The "real"
time, 4.8 seconds in this
case, is the amount of
actual time the program
took. This is the same
amount of time you
would have seen if you
stood there with a stop-
watch while the program
was running. "User time"
and "system time" show
the amount of time the
computer actually spent
on the process.

Some single commands actually spawn multiple processes.

On UNIX systems, you can apply the output of one command as the input to another, without creating an intermediary temporary file. We say that the output of one program is *piped* through another program (sometimes called a *filter*).

For example, suppose I want to search for all users logged in today who stayed logged in overnight. The *who* command shows me user names and what day they logged in:

```
% who
tanya      console Oct 19 09:30
lmui       ttyp0   Oct 18 15:58 (opal:0.0)
sybase     ttyp1   Oct 18 16:01 (rock.west.ora.co)
mam        ttyp2   Oct 19 13:03 (ncd12.ora.com:0.)
val        ttyp4   Oct 12 18:22 (harry.ora.com:0.)
   ...
```

Today is October 19. I might save this output in a file and then use the *-v* option to the *grep* command to search for all lines that do *not* have "Oct 19." So here's one way I might do what I want using two commands and one temporary file:

```
% who > who.out
% grep -v Oct 19 who.out
lmui       ttyp0   Oct 18 15:58 (opal:0.0)
sybase     ttyp1   Oct 18 16:01 (rock.west.ora.co)
val        ttyp4   Oct 12 18:22 (harry.ora.com:0.)
...
```

But I could also do this using one command and no temporary files, by just piping the output of *who* directly through the *grep* command.

```
% who | grep -v Oct 19
lmui       ttyp0   Oct 18 15:58 (opal:0.0)
sybase     ttyp1   Oct 18 16:01 (rock.west.ora.co)
val        ttyp4   Oct 12 18:22 (harry.ora.com:0.)
...
```

The advantage here is that it's faster, and that it doesn't require creating a temporary file that you then have to remove. However, it also means that you're running both the *who* and *grep* commands at once.

On a larger scale, at our office we have taken *troff* formatting to an art form, so that even the simplest *troff* file needs to run through a program called *soelim*, then through *sed*, *tbl*, and *sed* again, *awk*, *troff*, a *troff*-to-PostScript postprocessor, and finally *lpr* to print. We wrote a shell script for running all these commands together, called *fmat*. So when you run the *fmat* command just once, what really gets run is:

```
soelim <file> | sed -f /usr/txtools/sed/sedscr | tbl | troff
-Tps -mS -rz6 -rr1 -rv1 - | devps | lpr
```

Meanwhile, other programs run to save temporary files for creating a table of contents, an index, for saving error messages in case something goes wrong, and for embedding external PostScript figures into the document. So when you run this one shell script to create a *troff* file, you may think you're starting one process, but you're really starting a dozen.

Look for unwanted processes.

Usually, you know about all the processes you're running. However, occasionally, processes aren't properly killed when you think they are. For example, sometimes you might log out abnormally and processes associated with that terminal aren't completely killed.

When that happens, the processes just hang on, unassociated with a terminal, until the system is next booted or until you notice them and kill them yourself. Naturally, it's better to kill them yourself before they help bring the whole system to its knees.

For example, suppose I use the *ps* command to see what processes I'm running:

```
% ps
 PID TT STAT  TIME COMMAND
13745 q7 I     0:01 -csh (tcsh)
13781 q7 S     0:23 xlbiff
24912 q7 T     0:00 more ch01
23938 qe S     0:03 -csh (tcsh)
26079 qe S     0:00 xclock
26082 qe R     0:00 ps
```

The *more ch01* process was something that I didn't know I was running. At the time, I had accidentally run the *more* command in the background, which didn't work since *more* is an interactive program. I had gotten a message like this:

```
[1]  + Suspended (tty output) more ch01
```

Even though I got an error message, however, the process continued to run.

Set your clock by a slow down

When I worked in an old building with ancient electrical wiring, we'd sometimes have a power failure around 9:10 on a hot summer day. That's because everyone would come into the office, start up the coffee machines, turn on the lights, and start the AC, all at the same time.

The same thing can happen to our computer system. At around 9:10, people are all logging in, opening up their graphical email package, and starting a handful of xterm windows so they never have to wait for a command to complete. That can be a slow time.

Linda Lamb

You can stop processes with the kill command.

Sometimes you may see a process running that you don't want running anymore. The process may be an unwanted one that wasn't properly killed previously. Or maybe it's a process you put into the background and then reconsidered. Sometimes X programs don't give you an obvious way to exit. For example, the *xclock* program doesn't allow you to exit cleanly.

When you *do* have a way to exit a program cleanly, it's always better to stop the program that way instead. This is because programs usually have a cleanup procedure that they perform before exiting, and you want them to be able to complete it. For example, when you quit out of *vi*, it warns you if the file hasn't been written since the last change, and it removes its temporary files in */tmp*. If you kill *vi* externally, the latest changes are lost, and the temporary files remain on the system.

To kill a process, you can use the *kill* command. The one inconvenient thing about *kill* is that you need to tell it which process to kill, and usually the only way to do that is to use the process number. So you have to first use the *ps* command to get the process number. For example, suppose we want to kill the *more ch01* process shown below:

```
% ps
  PID TT STAT  TIME COMMAND
13745 q7 I     0:02 -csh (tcsh)
24912 q7 T     0:00 more ch01
26355 q7 R     0:00 ps
```

The process number is shown in the PID column (process ID). To kill the process, supply this number to the *kill* command:

```
% kill 24912
```

Then run *ps* again to make sure that the process was killed.

If the process wasn't killed, then you may need to use a stronger *kill level*. By default, *kill* works by sending the program a signal asking it to terminate. Some programs may ignore this signal. So if *kill* by itself doesn't work, try a stronger signal that can't be ignored, using the *kill –9* command.

```
% kill -9 24912
```

If the program you want to kill is an X program, there are other ways to do it. Many window managers have a "window menu" for each window, which among other things allow you to kill or close a window. Window managers may also have a "delete" or "destroy" selection on their root menu. In a pinch, you can also use the *xkill* command for X programs.

Job control makes killing programs a little easier.

If you're using a shell that supports job control (e.g., the C shell), then you don't have to track down the process IDs of programs you want to kill. Instead, you can use their job ID.

Use the *jobs* command to see all background processes currently running for your shell.

```
% jobs
[2]  - Running              xlbiff
[3]  + Suspended (tty output) more ch01
```

The number in the first column, surrounded by square brackets, is the job ID of the process. To kill one of these processes, just list the job ID, preceded by the percent sign (%). For example:

```
% kill %3
% jobs
[2]  + Running              xlbiff
```

Be aware of your resources.

It's dangerous when system administrators start lecturing about system resources, because users might think they should use the computer as little as possible. Although cutting back on use can be a good temporary strategy when conditions are particularly bad, it's not the philosophy to permanently embrace.

Think of the computer's resources as any other resource, such as tap water. Your tap water comes from a reservoir that has a limited amount of water in it. When there's a drought, you should stop sprinkling your lawn or taking long showers. But even when there isn't a drought, you don't leave the bathtub running all day.

It's the same idea with computer resources. Don't treat them like they're endless, because they aren't. You don't have to act like there's a drought all the time, but you should still treat your resources with respect.

What do you do when the system is slow?

I make some phone calls.

Jane Appleyard

Quick Reference

to space and time questions

Information to find and keep

Are there any naming conventions at your site for temporary files?

_____

_____

Are any files automatically deleted by the system? (e.g., those named *core*, those with a suffix of *.backup* or *.temp*, etc.)

_____

_____

What filesystems are available for user files on your system?

_____

_____

What changes are recommended when the system gets slow? Are there desktop accessories I should disable on an X terminal, applications I shouldn't run, maximum number of formatting jobs at one time, etc.?

_____

_____

_____

Look at space available and space used

See the disk space available on your system:

  % df

See how much space your home directory and subdirectories take up:

  % du ~

If you want only a grand total, use the *–s* option:

  % du -s

Look at how big the files are in a directory:

  % ls -l

Do rough comparisons and see which files are the largest.

Clean up your home directory to save space

1. Get in the habit of creating temporary files with distinctive names—such as names ending in *.temp* or *.tmp*, or names beginning with a comma—so that you can quickly delete files that don't matter.

2. Delete files named *core*.

3. Delete temporary files that weren't removed after they were created, such as files with a *.backup* suffix created by FrameMaker or files with a tilde suffix created by Emacs.

4. Delete files that you can easily recreate. For example, a graphic saved in two formats or PostScript files only needed for printing.

5. Delete messages that you don't need anymore. Sometimes the names of saved files are ambiguous. If you list files by date last modified you can see what files have not been changed in a long time. At our site, the command:

  % ls -lt

displays files by date modified.

6. Compress infrequently accessed files to save room. For example to compress the file *memo*, type:

  % compress memo

To compress all files in a directory, type:

  % compress *

To uncompress a file, type:

  % uncompress memo

"Write failed, filesystem is full!"

If you get this error while trying to save a file, the filesystem in which the file resides is full; e.g., if you are trying to save a file to /work/memo, this message means the filesystem /work is full.

1. Delete some files on the /work filesystem and then try to save the file.

2. Or, save the file to another filesystem. For example, if you know /home is separate from /work, save the file to ~/memo.

"No space left on device"

If there is no space in the directory used for edit buffers (e.g., /tmp or /usr/tmp):

1. Don't write the file. If you don't have multiple windows, remember that you can get a system prompt within the editor; e.g., in vi type:

    :!

2. Check in /usr/tmp with ls −l to see if there are any files there that belong to you.

3. Remove any unused files owned by you. If there aren't any such files, or if you're unsure, then you'll have to wait for the system administrator to clear up space. Be careful not to delete the file you're editing!

4. When there is space again, save your file.

When the system is slow

1. Look at your own processes:

    % ps -x

2. Identify resource hogs:

- Displays that constantly update themselves (like xload or top)

- Processes that are unwanted

- Processes running in the background

- Graphical programs (especially if you have a text alternative)

- Commands that spawn multiple processes like commands to format troff files

3. Kill processes by number; e.g., if process number 24912 shown by a ps command is not needed, type:

    % kill 24912

Or, if your environment supports job control, you can use the jobs command to look for running jobs:

    % jobs

and kill the job number in the first column (preceded by a % sign):

    % kill %3

CHAPTER 7

What you need to know about everyone else

UNIX is a multiuser system; you can find out what other users are doing.

On a typical UNIX system, many users will all be sharing the same machine. Occasionally you might want to find out some very basic information. Is a coworker logged in yet? Has he or she read the email you sent late last night? If users never log out, how do you know when they come in to work in the morning? You can find out quite a lot about the other users and about the system as a whole, without any special permissions.

This may sound like snooping. And technically it is. But it's legitimate snooping—sort of the equivalent of looking at who your roommates got mail from, without actually opening the envelopes.

By looking at what others are doing, you can also get a better sense of the system as a whole. This chapter explains:

- How to find out who's logged in, and what they're doing
- How to learn someone's login name
- How to learn who is on a mail alias

Finding people

Sometimes, you just want to know if someone is in the office or if they're at some conference for the week. Some people set up their email and voice mail so that anyone who tries to contact them will get this kind of information. Other people leave you guessing.

Arsenio Santos

You can find out who is logged in.

If you want to find out who's currently logged in on the system (and what time they logged in), use the *who* command:

```
% who
root console Sep 26 17:01
lmui ttyp0 Sep 26 17:47 (harry.ora.com:0.)
eap  ttyp2 Sep 23 13:54 (nugget.west.ora.)
jhm  ttyp3 Sep 24 06:00 (fudge.rtr.com)
mam  ttyp4 Sep 27 07:11 (ncd12.ora.com:0.)
     ...
```

For each user, the *who* command reports what terminal device they're logged in on, when they logged in, and where they logged in from.

Use who with the more or grep command to find out if a particular user is logged in.

On systems with many users, *who* may produce too much output to be easily scanned. You can pipe the *who* command through *more* if you want to be able to scan the output:

```
% who | more
```

You can also check to see if a particular user is logged in by piping the output through the *grep* command. For example, to find out if *frank* is logged in:

```
% who | grep frank
frank ttyq9 Sep 27 10:08 (ncd1.ora.com:0.0)
frank ttyqc Sep 27 10:08 (ncd1.ora.com:0.0)
```

Frank logged in at 10:08 this morning, with two terminal windows.

Remember to take this information with a grain of salt. For example, just because people are logged in to the computer doesn't mean that they're on the premises. I never log out, so someone typing *who* at 3:30 AM will see me logged in. Now, I may work hard upon occasion, but I'm not nuts.

You may want to sort your output

The order that *who* reports information isn't very meaningful to most of us. Sometimes you may be more interested in seeing who's logged in, in alphabetical order. To do that, use the *sort* command.

```
% who | sort
andyo  ttyr0 ...
bobbi  ttys7 ...
bobbi  ttys8 ...
bonnie ttyu3 ...
bradley ttyq8 ...
...
```

You can find out what other users are doing with ps.

The *ps* command shows you processes that are running on the system. Usually, you use *ps* just to learn what you're doing, but you can also use it to show all processes, or all processes associated with another user. So you can use *ps* to find out who's doing what.

The options to *ps* are very system-dependent. But on our system (which is BSD–based), I can see what other users are doing using the *ps –au* command. (I pipe the output through *more* because *ps* typically shows screenfuls and screenfuls of output.) On a System V–based system, I would use *ps –ef* instead.

```
% ps -au | more
USER   PID   %CPU %MEM  SZ  RSS TT STAT START  TIME COMMAND
len    18217 29.7  0.9  740 1040 s4 R   10:46  0:00 gtroff
ellen  18205 24.2  0.6  240  756 q5 R   10:45  0:04 perl -- #
bobbi  16257  0.0  0.2  188  264 s7 I   10:15  0:00 -csh
val    15290  0.0  0.1   48  120 q4 I   14:52  0:00 less
val     5993  0.0  0.1   92  172 q9 I   Oct 18 0:00 -sh
dom    16451  0.0  0.1   48  100 s5 I   10:22  0:00 rlogin rock
fred     653  0.0  0.1  216  156 p4 I   Oct 12 0:02 spider
```

Len is running *gtroff*, Ellen is running *perl*, Dom is logged in to another machine called *rock*, and Fred (the deadbeat!) is playing an X-based game called *spider*. (Actually, today is October 20, and *ps* tells me that *spider* has been running since October 12, so it's most likely that Fred iconified the window and just forgot about it.)

Administrators are the ones who are most likely to use *ps* to keep an eye on all users on the system. If the system is really slow, administrators may run *ps* to see if there are people running games or any programs that look "hung."

Use grep with ps to see what a single person is doing.

On most systems with multiple users, the output from a *ps –au* command is screenfuls upon screenfuls. Usually, you're only interested in a particular thing—such as, what is a particular user doing, or is anyone running a particular program right now?

Hidden agenda

I sent out mail to our office on how to do:

who | sort | more

to check on how many logins you currently had.

I was secretly hoping (since the system was very slow) that people with seven logins would realize that everyone could see what they were doing, be embarrassed at the exposure of their own excessive use of resources, and would change their behavior.

It worked, with a few people.

Linda Lamb

On some systems, there may be a special option to *ps* for other users. Check your *ps* manpage. If there's no such option on your system, then pipe the *ps* output through *grep*. For example, if I only want to know what *frank* is up to:

```
% ps -au | grep frank
frank    29887    176 p9 I    Oct 17  0:00 -sh (csh)
frank    29886    176 pa I    Oct 17  0:00 -sh (csh)
lmui     19574    236 s6 S    10:55   0:00 egrep frank
```

ps usually reports only the processes associated with a terminal. Not all processes are associated with a terminal. If you want to see all processes belonging to Frank, add the *x* command-line option:

```
% ps -aux | grep frank
frank 29850  284 ?  I  Oct 17  0:02 /usr/vue/bin/vuesession
frank 29887  176 p9 I  Oct 17  0:00 -sh (csh)
lmui  19761  236 s6 S  10:57   0:00 egrep frank
frank 29885  360 ?  S  Oct 17  0:03 xload -name vueload -no1
frank 29886  176 pa I  Oct 17  0:00 -sh (csh)
frank 29873  808 ?  S  Oct 17  0:45 vuewm
frank 29900 2148 ?  S  Oct 17 12:04 /usr/lib/Zmail/bin/zmail
frank 29876  164 p6 I  Oct 17  0:00 /usr/softbench/bin/softm
```

The finger command shows you how long terminals have been idle.

The *finger* command can also show you who's logged in, and the output is a little more friendly. For example, if I run *finger* without any arguments, I see all users listed:

```
% finger
-User-    --Full name--    -What- Idle TTY -Console Location-
andyo     Andy Oram        bash-1 2:05 r0  ncd13 (X display 0)
bobbi     Bobbi Kraham     tcsh      1 s7  ncd20 (X display 0)
                           tcsh     40 s8  ncd20 (X display 0)
bonnie    Bonnie Hyland    xemacs       u3 ncd32 (X display 0)
```

finger doesn't just tell you who's logged in, it also tells you their full name, what program is currently active in that terminal window, and how long they've been *idle* in that window (if at all).

Like *who*, *finger* only pays attention to terminal shells. So when it says someone has been idle for five hours in each of her terminals, that really doesn't tell you very much. For example, since I've been doing all my work today in FrameMaker and with my graphical mail program, anyone checking my idle time will probably think that I haven't done anything for hours. *finger* doesn't know that I've been typing madly in my FrameMaker window all afternoon.

Finger shows when other users last read their email.

finger can also tell you when the person last read his or her email. For example, if you run *finger* on a single user, you'll get some extra information about him, including whether he's been reading his mail:

```
% finger frank
Login name: frank In real life: Frank Willison
Directory: /ruby/home/frank Shell: /bin/csh
On since Oct 17 08:09:28 on ttyp9 from ncd1.ora.com:0.0
3 hours 22 minutes Idle Time
Mail last read Thu Oct 20 16:19:04 1994
No Plan.

Login name: frank In real life: Frank Willison
Directory: /ruby/home/frank Shell: /bin/csh
On since Oct 17 08:09:28 on ttypa from ncd1.ora.com:0.0
2 days 1 hour Idle Time
```

Frank's read his email in the past hour (which means he has no excuse not to have responded to my last message).

Your *finger* output may vary. For example, on another machine, *finger*'s output looks more like this:

```
% finger frank
-User-     --Full name--   -What- Idle TTY -Console Location-
frank      Frank Willison  csh    3:23 p9  ncd1 (X display 0)
                           csh    2d1h pa  ncd1 (X display 0)
  [387,100]  </ruby/home/frank>;  Group: ora
  Groups: production

  frank has no new mail, last read Thu 20-Oct-94 4:19PM
```

You can use the finger command to find out what people are doing on other systems.

You can only run the *who* or *ps* commands on a machine if you can log in to that machine. Not so with the *finger* command. You can use *finger* on a remote machine just as easily;

you just have to precede the machine name with an at sign (@). For example, if I want to see what's going on at a remote machine called *rock*, I can run *finger* on that machine:

```
% finger @rock.west.ora.com
[rock.west.ora.com]
Trying 198.112.209.1...
rock -- Home of ORA-WEST 1-800-998-9938
 12:12pm  up 4 days, 11:46,  59 users,  load average: 4.80,
5.51, 5.19

-User-  --Full name--   -What-  Idle  TTY -Console Location-
abbot  Abbot Chambers    pine      2  p9   xterm36 (X Window)
                         tcsh   1:40  q3   xterm36 (X Window)
                         pico      6  s8   xterm36 (X Window)
allen  Allen Noren        vi      32  p5   xterm23 (X Window)
                          csh   2:03  s6   xterm23 (X Window)
                       xmosai   2:03  s7   xterm23 (X Window)
                          csh     34  t4   xterm23 (X Window)
andrea Andrea Reust       csh   2:16  pb   xterm32 (X Window)
ann    Ann Lennon         csh   3:45  qe   xterm31 (X Window)
    ...
```

Not all sites support *finger*, so this may not work for all systems. But it works on *rock*. Even though I have an account on *rock*, using *finger* is faster than logging in remotely and running *who*.

I can also look at what a single user is doing on a remote machine, by specifying their name followed by an at sign followed by the hostname (i.e., similar to an email address on the Internet). For example, let's see what my father-in-law at MIT is up to. (His login name and machine name have been changed to protect his dignity.)

```
% finger dan@atom.mit.edu
[atom.mit.edu]
Trying 18.62.1.73...
Login name: dan In real life: Dan K.
Directory: /u/dan Shell: /bin/csh
On since Oct 20 07:58:49 on console 261 days Idle Time
Plan:
    ...

Login name: dan In real life: Dan K.
Directory: /u/dan Shell: /bin/csh
On since Oct 20 11:20:21 on ttyp3 1 hour 15 minutes Idle Time
...
```

I'm sparing you the screenfuls of output. But from this, I found out that my father-in-law has at least one window in which he worked today, which means he's in town this week and not off at a physicists' convention or whatever it is they do.

Notice that although you use the same sort of syntax that you would for an email address, you can't assume that any email address will work. In fact, many email addresses won't, since many sites have a policy of not giving out real login names for email addresses, just mail aliases. The email address I give out to people is *Linda.Mui@ora.com*, but if people try using *finger* on this address, *finger* won't know who I am.

You can use finger to find out someone's login name.

What if you don't know someone's login name? *finger* is sometimes smart enough to find users from only their first name or a portion of their name. For example, if someone were looking for me, only knowing that my name was Linda Mui and I worked at *ora.com*, he or she might type:

```
% finger mui@ora.com
```

and see:

```
[ora.com]
Login name: lmui  In real life: Linda Mui
Directory: /home/lmui  Shell: /bin/tcsh
On since Oct 20 09:43:14 on ttyr5 from opal:0.0
7 minutes 14 seconds Idle Time
Mail last read Thu Oct 20 15:06:24 1994
No Plan.

Login name: peter  In real life: Peter Mui
Directory: /home/peter  Shell: /bin/tcsh
Last login Thu Oct 20 08:33 on ttyqa from ora-east-nb.ora.
New mail received Thu Oct 20 15:51:38 1994;
   unread since Thu Oct 20 08:33:25 1994
No Plan.
```

From here, you can tell that there are two Muis with accounts at *ora.com*, me and my brother Peter. And my login name is *lmui*.

Don't believe finger when it tells you when someone last logged in.

If you *finger* a user who isn't currently logged in, *finger* tells you when last he or she was logged in. Theoretically, this

Do you ever use finger?

I use finger all the time to see if someone is in the California office when you only get their voice mail. Especially now that our California office has two buildings and all these new people, the receptionist has no idea who the person is, much less if they're in yet.

Sometimes I use finger to see if anyone has a neat .plan file. Sometimes I can tell that someone else has fingered me, like this friend of mine I haven't talked to in a long time and suddenly he sends me mail about this poem I put in my .plan file because I thought it was cool.

Jane Appleyard

would come in useful when you want to know if someone came in over the weekend. If it worked, that is.

```
% finger donna
Login name: donna In real life: Donna Woonteiler
Directory: /home/donna Shell: /bin/csh
Last login Wed Aug 11, 1993 on ttyp2 from rock.west.ora.co
New mail received Thu Oct 20 12:57:37 1994;
   unread since Sat Jun 11 10:39:17 1994
No Plan.
```

Here's the rub: this information may be very wrong. If people use *xterm* windows, then the information on when they last logged in may not be properly registered with the system. So actually, the information in the above example is completely wrong. Donna was logged in as recently as June 1994, but the last login remembered by UNIX was one in August 1993 when she logged in via a terminal connection.

Some users have a .plan file to tell others what they're up to.

Among other things, the *finger* command looks for a file in your home directory called *.plan*. You can use this file to tell people more about yourself—for example, to tell them what your responsibilities are, what your office extension is, and to amuse them with your witticisms.

If you don't have a *.plan* file, then all *finger* reports is "No Plan." But if you create a file called *.plan* in your home directory, then *finger* will find and print that file. For example, I created a *.plan* file reading:

```
          Hours: 9:30 to 6PM EST (approx.)
Phone extension: x466
Off-hours phone number: 555-5466
```

In addition, *finger* looks in a *.project* file for a single line describing your current project. For example, I might have a *.project* file containing this line:

```
What Users Need to know about UNIX Sysadm
```

(Any additional lines in *.project* are ignored.)

The *.plan* and *.project* files need to be readable by all users, and your home directory must be executable for all users. So run the following commands:

```
% chmod a+r .plan .project
```

```
% chmod a+x .
```

When someone runs *finger* on me now, they'll see:

```
Login name: lmui  In real life: Linda Mui
Directory: /home/lmui  Shell: /bin/tcsh
On since Oct 21 09:58:38 on ttyq7 from opal:0.0
Mail last read Fri Oct 21 10:52:41 1994
Project: What Users Need to know about UNIX Sysadm
Plan:
Hours:  9:30 to 6PM EST (approximately)
Phone extension: x466
Off-hours phone number: 555-5466
```

You should be careful about what sort of information you put in *.project* and *.plan*, since they can be read by anyone over the Internet. Unless your company is protected from the outside world via a firewall, it isn't a good idea to mention a company project that hasn't been announced yet in your *.plan* file.

You can find out who is on a mail alias.

Most computerized offices have mail "aliases" for groups of people in a single department, or groups of people with a particular interest. At our office, we have groups called *writers*, *editors*, *managers*, *sales*, *marketing*, and *production*, for various departments throughout the company. We also have groups for people invested into our 401k program, people who take public transportation to work, and people who use Macintosh computers. And all employees belong to *ora*, a group for the entire company.

On UNIX machines that use *sendmail*, these aliases are defined in a file called */etc/aliases* or */usr/lib/aliases*. It's useful to be able to track down an alias if you want to know who mail is going to before you send it out. The *aliases* file is the place to start if you want to trace an alias.

For example, if someone wanted to know who was on the *writers* alias, he or she might look for this line:

```
writers: eap, paula, lmui, val, jerry, tim
```

There are six people on the writer's alias, and I'm one of them. The quick way to get this information is to just *grep* through the *aliases* file:

Using the .plan file

I try to keep my .plan file up-to-date. There's no point describing what I do there—that's either too static or too dynamic to be useful, depending on how you look at it, but I do keep my schedule in there.

A .plan file is a good publicly-accessible place to note what you'll be doing and when. I learned to use it while I was a graduate student at UMass, where we all kept our class and research schedules in our .plan files. That way if someone came into the lab looking for a colleague, it was easy to look and see when you could expect him/her to be around.

I also use a WWW [World Wide Web] home page to let people know about myself and my plans.

Norman Walsh

Alternatives to .plan

I have other, better, ways of revealing my personality than a .plan file—like my Web page or email correspondence.

Arsenio Santos

```
% grep writers /etc/aliases
# All the known writers, that are employed by ORA
writers: eap, paula, lmui, val, jerry, tim
```

In addition to user names, an alias might also list a filename. In that case, the mail is not only sent to any users listed, but it is also archived in the specified file.

Quick Reference

to finding out about other people

Information to find and keep

What options to the *ps* command are supported on your system?

All processes by all users: _____

_____

_____

_____

All processes by a particular user: _____

_____

_____

_____

Include processes not associated with a terminal:

_____

_____

_____

Find out who is logged on

To see who is currently logged in on your system, and what time they logged in, type:

```
%  who
```

Pipe the output through more, if there is more than one screenful of users:

```
% who | more
```

See if a particular user is logged on; e.g., to see if the user *frank* is logged on:

```
% who | grep frank
```

Find out when people last read email

See when users last read their mail; e.g., to see when the user *frank* on your system last read mail, type:

```
% finger frank
```

What people are doing on other systems

Use the *finger* command with the name of the remote machine; e.g., to see activity on a machine with the name *rock.west.ora.com*, type:

```
% finger @rock.west.ora.com
```

See what a single user is doing, if you know that user's login name and address:

```
% finger frank@rock.west.ora.com
```

Finger does not always report reliable information. Also, some sites disable *finger* for security reasons.

Create a .plan file

If you have *.plan* or *.project* files, people can learn more about you when they use *finger*.

1. Use a text editor to create a file called *.plan* in your home directory. You can include contact information, job title, etc. You can also create a one-line file named *.project* in your home directory.

   ```
   % cd
   % vi .plan
   ```
   or
   ```
   % emacs .plan
   ```

2. Make the *.plan* and *.project* files readable by all users, and your home directory executable for all users.

   ```
   % chmod a+r .plan .project
   % chmod a+x .
   ```

See who is on a mail alias

1. Look in the */etc/aliases* file.

   ```
   % more /etc/aliases
   ```

2. If you have the *verify* command on your system, you can use that; e.g., to verify users on the *sales* alias, type:

   ```
   % verify sales
   ```

   If the alias is not stored locally, give the full address:

   ```
   % verify sales@ora.com
   ```

What you need to know if you need to know more

Some readers may want to know more.

As we said in the *Preface*, this book is aimed at readers who aren't interested much in computers, but just in getting their work done. Some readers, however, may get to the end of the book and find that they want to know more. We've tried to cover everything we could, but maybe you need some details we left out for the sake of clarity. Maybe your UNIX system is configured differently (for example, some systems enforce more elaborate file permissions than standard UNIX permissions). Since we don't go into much detail about individual programs, maybe you need to know more about doing queries on a relational database, or how to fix a *troff* file.

Or maybe after reading this book, you no longer think of UNIX as something conceptually out of your grasp. Maybe you're just itching to learn a little bit more, because you realize that there isn't as much to it as you thought. We said in the *Preface* that we weren't going to try to get you to like UNIX, but deep down we hope that you're a little more comfortable with it after reading this book.

There's no substitute for asking your neighbor.

Don't get me wrong; I like books. But I'd always rather have someone explain something to me in person.

It's like when you're driving someplace you've never been before. I don't mind looking at a map, but I prefer to have someone in the car who can show me the best way to get there. You can see from the map that you want to make a left onto Elm Street, but only someone who knows the way can tell you that you can't make that left turn between 4 PM and 6 PM, or that it's the first left after a gas station, or that you can make an earlier turn and avoid the traffic light.

The best resource for any information is to ask someone who knows. If you have an officemate or coworker who doesn't mind being asked to help, you've struck gold.

Read reference pages (manpages) when available.

Practically every program comes with a manpage describing what it does and what command-line options it supports. Manpages also list bugs, caveats (a.k.a., more bugs), related files, related commands, and examples. Although manpages are sometimes difficult to read (they are usually written by programmers), they are also one of the best sources for knowing what the program can do.

Use the man command to read manpages on your system. See Chapter 3 for more information.

Look for system documentation.

Many users think that UNIX comes without any documentation. Often there is a complete documentation set, but usually only one copy per site, which your administrator keeps. If your administrator has system documentation, she might be persuaded to lend it to you. (Although you shouldn't be offended if your administrator makes you read it in her office—since there's only one copy, administrators are often wary of losing it).

Look for "Frequently Asked Questions" lists.

A Frequently Asked Questions (FAQ) list is a collection of common questions concerning a general topic, with the answers included. Many FAQ lists come out of USENET, a set of "newsgroups" (similar to bulletin boards) about practically every topic under the sun. In addition to newsgroups in which people around the world discuss their pets or favorite TV programs, there are many groups about computers.

There are several ways to find the FAQ for a particular topic. If you have USENET news, look in the relevant newsgroup for an FAQ list at the beginning of the month, when most FAQs are reposted. You can also try the special group *news.answers*, on which many FAQ lists are cross-posted. If you don't know how to read USENET news at your site, ask a coworker or ask your administrator.

A good catch-all newsgroup for UNIX questions is *comp.unix.questions*. Many common UNIX questions can be found in the FAQ list for that group.

If your site doesn't receive USENET newsgroups, you might still be able to get the FAQ list for a group. You can use FTP or a World Wide Web browser to find FAQ lists. Ask your administrator for assistance.

Ask complete strangers.

If your site has a USENET feed, then you can try "posting" your questions to a newsgroup. Before you post, you should make a concentrated effort to read any manpages, manuals, and FAQ lists. When you're sure that your question isn't answered in any of those places, post the question to the appropriate newsgroup (such as *comp.unix.questions*). You can use the *postnews* command, or post directly from your newsreader.

Buy (or borrow) books.

Our company's business is publishing, so perhaps it's self-serving to tell you to buy books. But if you can't find your answers anywhere else, it's possible that you can find a book that helps. We recommend the following books:

McGilton, Henry and Rachel Morgan. *Introducing the UNIX System*. New York: McGraw-Hill, 1983. 556 pp. A good conceptual introduction to UNIX. The book that I (and everyone I know) learned UNIX from.

Peek, Jerry, Tim O'Reilly, and Mike Loukides. *UNIX Power Tools*. Sebastopol, CA: O'Reilly & Associates, Inc., 1993. 1162 pp. A collection of tips, tricks, and instruction about UNIX. Includes a CD-ROM. For technically-adept new users and seasoned pros.

Frisch, Æleen. *Essential System Administration*. Sebastopol, CA: O'Reilly & Associates, Inc., 1991. 466 pp. An introduction to UNIX system administration. Geared towards administrators, but also useful if you just want to learn how the system ticks.

Lamb, Linda and Jerry Peek. *What You Need To Know About Using Email Effectively*. Sebastopol, CA: O'Reilly & Associates, Inc., 1995. 146 pp. Tips for using email effectively, geared towards nontechnical users.

Index

& (ampersand), 106
* (asterisk), 28, 50
. (period; dot)
   as a command, 36
   in filenames, 50
@ (at sign), 121–124
\ (backslash), 37, 50
_ (underscore), 50
| (pipe; vertical bar), 50, 110–111

accounts, disabled, 23
administrators
   changing
      file ownership, 62
      permissions, 58
   getting help from, 5–13
   keeping backup files, 103
   monitoring users, 119
   recovering passwords, 25
   responsibilities of, 3–5
alias command, 38
aliases, 38–41
   mail, 125
   setting for printers, 80
applications (see programs)
apropos command, 42, 45

ASCII
   file format, 73
   terminals, 18–19

background processes, 106
backup files, 102, 103
.bashrc file, 36–37, 39
Berkeley Standard Distribution (BSD)
   systems, 38
   groups on, 54
   output of df, 93
   printing, 72, 79–85
bin directories, 33–37
binary format, 33
bit syntax, permission, 63, 64
Bourne shell, 39
bypassing .xsession file, 28

C shell, 39
cables, electric, 17
cancel command, 84–85
cancelling
   jobs, 34
   printing, 84–85
case sensitivity, 21, 32, 33, 50
   of passwords, 27

About the Author

Linda Mui began working in UNIX in 1985. She didn't know an operating system from her elbow, but she eventually learned UNIX by looking over other peoples' shoulders. She worked in system administration for two years before she began writing for a living.

Although no longer working in system administration, Linda remains a resource whenever users have trouble. She has been called "The UNIX Lone Ranger," roaming office hallways looking for users in need of assistance.

In addition to *What You Need To Know When You Can't Find Your UNIX System Administrator*, Linda has written or coauthored *termcap & terminfo*, *Pick Basic*, *The X Window System Administrator's Guide*, and *X User Tools*. She lives in Cambridge, Massachusetts.

Colophon

Our look is the result of reader comments, our own experimentation, and feedback from distribution channels. Distinctive covers complement our distinctive approach to technical topics, breathing personality and life into potentially dry subjects.

In the What You Need to Know series, we look at technology in a personal way: how real people get something done and how they think about issues. The covers of the series reflect this personal, immediate approach to the subject. Inside the books, illustrations of the speakers in the sidebars give faces to those who have shared their experiences.

Edie Freedman designed the cover of this book, using an illustration by David White, in the style of 19th-century engravings. The cover layout was produced with Quark XPress 3.3 using the ITC Garamond and Futura fonts.

The inside layout was designd by Jennifer Niederst and implemented in FrameMaker 3.0 by Mike Sierra. The text and heading fonts are set in the ITC Garamond and Garamond Condensed families. The sidebar text and headings are set in the Gill Sans font. The portraits were illustrated by Leslie Evans.

USING
UNIX AND X

Books from O'Reilly & Associates, Inc.

FALL/WINTER 1994-95

–Basics–

Our UNIX in a Nutshell *guides are the most comprehensive quick reference on the market—a must for every* UNIX *user. No matter what system you use, we've got a version to cover your needs.*

UNIX in a Nutshell: System V Edition

By Daniel Gilly & the staff of O'Reilly & Associates
2nd Edition June 1992
444 pages, ISBN 1-56592-001-5

You may have seen UNIX quick-reference guides, but you've never seen anything like *UNIX in a Nutshell*. Not a scaled-down quick reference of common commands, *UNIX in a Nutshell* is a complete reference containing all commands and options, along with generous descriptions and examples that put the commands in context. For all but the thorniest UNIX problems, this one reference should be all the documentation you need. Covers System V, Releases 3 and 4, and Solaris 2.0.

"This book is the perfect desktop reference.... The authors have presented a clear and concisely written book which would make an excellent addition to any UNIX user's library."
—*SysAdmin*

"Whether you are setting up your first UNIX system or adding your fiftieth user, these books can ease you through learning the fundamentals of the UNIX system."
—Michael J. O'Brien, Hardware Editor,
  ABA/Unix/group Newsletter

SCO UNIX in a Nutshell

By Ellie Cutler & the staff of O'Reilly & Associates
1st Edition February 1994
590 pages, ISBN 1-56592-037-6

The desktop reference to SCO UNIX and Open Desktop®, this version of *UNIX in a Nutshell* shows you what's under the hood of your SCO system. It isn't a scaled-down quick reference of common commands, but a complete reference containing all user, programming, administration, and networking commands.

Contents include:
- All commands and options
- Shell syntax for the Bourne, Korn, C, and SCO shells
- Pattern matching, with *vi, ex, sed*, and *aw*k commands
- Compiler and debugging commands for software development
- Networking with email, TCP/IP, NFS, and UUCP
- System administration commands and the SCO sysadmsh shell

This edition of *UNIX in a Nutshell* is the most comprehensive SCO quick reference on the market, a must for any SCO user. You'll want to keep *SCO UNIX in a Nutshell* close by as you use your computer: it'll become a handy, indispensible reference for working with your SCO system.

Learning the UNIX Operating System

By Grace Todino, John Strang & Jerry Peek
3rd Edition August 1993
108 pages, ISBN 1-56592-060-0

If you are new to UNIX, this concise introduction will tell you just what you need to get started and no more. Why wade through a 600-page book when you can begin working productively in a matter of minutes? It's an ideal primer for Mac and PC users of the Internet who need to know a little bit about UNIX on the systems they visit.

Topics covered include:

- Logging in and logging out
- Window systems (especially X/Motif)
- Managing UNIX files and directories
- Sending and receiving mail
- Redirecting input/output
- Pipes and filters
- Background processing
- Basic network commands

This book is the most effective introduction to UNIX in print. The third edition has been updated and expanded to provide increased coverage of window systems and networking. It's a handy book for someone just starting with UNIX, as well as someone who encounters a UNIX system as a visitor via remote login over the Internet.

"Once you've established a connection with the network, there's often a secondary obstacle to surmount.... *Learning the UNIX Operating System* helps you figure out what to do next by presenting in a nutshell the basics of how to deal with the 'U-word.' Obviously a 92-page book isn't going to make you an instant UNIX guru, but it does an excellent job of introducing basic operations in a concise nontechnical way, including how to navigate through the file system, send and receive E-mail and—most importantly—get to the online help...."
—Michael L. Porter, Associate Editor, *Personal Engineering & Instrumentation News*

"Whether you are setting up your first UNIX system or adding your fiftieth user, [this book] can ease you through learning the fundamentals of the UNIX system."
—Michael J. O'Brien, *ABA/Unix/group Newsletter*

Learning the vi Editor

By Linda Lamb
5th Edition October 1990
192 pages, ISBN 0-937175-67-6

A complete guide to text editing with *vi*, the editor available on nearly every UNIX system. Early chapters cover the basics; later chapters explain more advanced editing tools, such as *ex* commands and global search and replacement.

"For those who are looking for an introductory book to give to new staff members who have no acquaintance with either screen editing or with UNIX screen editing, this is it: a book on *vi* that is neither designed for the UNIX in-crowd, nor so imbecilic that one is ashamed to use it."
—*;login*

Learning the Korn Shell

By Bill Rosenblatt
1st Edition June 1993
363 pages, ISBN 1-56592-054-6

A thorough introduction to the Korn shell, both as a user interface and as a programming language. This book provides a clear explanation of the Korn shell's features, including *ksh* string operations, co-processes, signals and signal handling, and command-line interpretation. *Learning the Korn Shell* also includes real-life programming examples and a Korn shell debugger (*kshdb*).

"Readers still bending back the pages of Korn-shell manuals will find relief in...*Learning the Korn Shell*...a gentle introduction to the shell. Rather than focusing on syntax issues, the book quickly takes on the task of solving day-to-day problems with Korn-shell scripts. Application scripts are also shown and explained in detail. In fact, the book even presents a script debugger written for *ksh*. This is a good book for improving your knowledge of the shell."
—*Unix Review*

MH & xmh: E-mail for Users & Programmers

By Jerry Peek
2nd Edition September 1992
728 pages, ISBN 1-56592-027-9

Customizing your email environment can save time and make communicating more enjoyable. *MH & xmh: E-Mail for Users & Programmers* explains how to use, customize, and program with the MH electronic mail commands available on virtually any UNIX system. The handbook also covers *xmh*, an X Window System client that runs MH programs.

The second edition added a chapter on *mhook*, sections explaining under-appreciated small commands and features, and more examples showing how to use MH to handle common situations.

"The MH bible is irrefutably Jerry Peek's *MH & xmh: E-mail for Users & Programmers*. This book covers just about everything that is known about MH and *xmh* (the X Windows front end to MH), presented in a clear and easy-to-read format. I strongly recommend that anybody serious about MH get a copy."
—James Hamilton, *UnixWorld*

Learning the GNU Emacs

By Debra Cameron & Bill Rosenblatt
1st Edition October 1991
442 pages, ISBN 0-937175-84-6

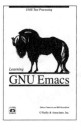

An introduction to the GNU Emacs editor, one of the most widely used and powerful editors available under UNIX. Provides a solid introduction to basic editing, a look at several important editing modes (special Emacs features for editing specific types of documents), and a brief introduction to customization and Emacs LISP programming. The book is aimed at new Emacs users, whether or not they are programmers.

"Authors Debra Cameron and Bill Rosenblatt do a particularly admirable job presenting the extensive functionality of GNU Emacs in well-organized, easily digested chapters.... Despite its title, *Learning GNU Emacs* could easily serve as a reference for the experienced Emacs user."
—Linda Branagan, Convex Computer Corporation

The USENET Handbook

By Mark Harrison
1st Edition Winter 1994-95 (est.)
250 pages (est.), ISBN 1-56592-101-1

The USENET Handbook describes how to get the most out of the USENET news network, a worldwide network of cooperating computer sites that exchange public user messages known as "articles" or "postings." These postings are an electric mix of questions, commentary, hints, and ideas of all kinds, expressing the views of the thousands of participants at these sites.

Tutorials show you how to read news using the most popular newsreaders—*tin* and Trumpet for Windows and *nn*, *emacs* and *gnus* for UNIX. It also explains how to post articles to the Net.

The book discusses things you can do to increase your productivity by using the resources mentioned on USENET, such as anonymous FTP (file transfer protocol), mail servers, FAQs, and mailing lists. It covers network etiquette, processing encoded and compressed files (i.e., software, pictures, etc.), and lots of historical information.

Using UUCP and Usenet

By Grace Todino & Dale Dougherty
1st Edition February 1986 (latest update October 1991)
210 pages, ISBN 0-937175-10-2

Shows users how to communicate with both UNIX and non-UNIX systems using UUCP and *cu* or *tip* and how to read news and post articles. This handbook assumes that UUCP is already running at your site.

"Are you having trouble with UUCP? Have you torn out your hair trying to set the Dialers file? *Managing UUCP and Usenet* and *Using UUCP and Usenet* will give you the information you need to become an accomplished net user. The companion book is *!%@:: A Directory of Electronic Mail Addressing & Networks*, a compendium of world networks and how to address and read them. All of these books are well written, and I urge you to take a look at them."
—*Root Journal*

X User Tools

By Linda Mui & Valerie Quercia
1st Edition October 1994 (est.)
750 pages (est.) (CD-ROM included)
ISBN 1-56592-019-8

 *X User Tools* provides for X users what *UNIX Power Tools* provides for UNIX users: hundreds of tips, tricks, scripts, techniques, and programs—plus a CD-ROM—to make the X Windowing System more enjoyable, more powerful, and easier to use.

This browser's book emphasizes useful programs, culled from the network and contributed by X programmers worldwide. Programs range from fun (games, screensavers, and a variety of online clocks) to business tools (calendar, memo, and mailer programs) to graphics (programs for drawing, displaying, and converting images). You'll also find a number of tips and techniques for configuring both individual and systemwide environments, as well as a glossary of common X and UNIX terms.

The browser style of organization—pioneered by *UNIX Power Tools*—encourages readers to leaf through the book at will, focusing on what appeals at the time. Each article stands on its own, many containing cross-references to related articles. Before you know it, you'll have covered the entire book, simply by scanning what's of interest and following cross-references to more detailed information.

The enclosed CD-ROM contains source files for all and binary files for some of the programs—for a number of platforms, including Sun 4, Solaris, HP 700, Alpha/OSF, and AIX. Note that the CD-ROM contains software for both *emacs* and *tcl/tk*.

Volume 3: X Window System User's Guide

Standard Edition
By Valerie Quercia & Tim O'Reilly
4th Edition May 1993
836 pages, ISBN 1-56592-014-7

 *The X Window System User's Guide* orients the new user to window system concepts and provides detailed tutorials for many client programs, including the *xterm* terminal emulator and window managers. Building on this basic knowledge, later chapters explain how to customize the X environment and provide sample configurations. The *Standard Edition* uses the *twm* manager in most examples and illustrations. Revised for X11 Release 5. This popular manual is available in two editions, one for users of the MIT software, and one for users of Motif. (see below).

"For the novice, this is the best introduction to X available. It will also be a convenient reference for experienced users and X applications developers."
—*Computing Reviews*

Volume 3M: X Window System User's Guide

Motif Edition
By Valerie Quercia & Tim O'Reilly
2nd Edition January 1993
956 pages, ISBN 1-56592-015-5

This alternative edition of the *User's Guide* highlights the Motif window manager for users of the Motif graphical user interface. Revised for Motif 1.2 and X11 Release 5.

Material covered in this second edition includes:

- Overview of the X Color Management System (Xcms)

- Creating your own Xcms color database

- Tutorials for two "color editors": *xcoloredit* and *xtici*

- Using the X font server

- Tutorial for *editres*, a resource editor

- Extensive coverage of the new implementations of *bitmap* and *xmag*

- Overview of internationalization features

- Features common to Motif 1.2 applications: tear-off menus and drag-and-drop

–Advanced–

UNIX Power Tools

By Jerry Peek, Mike Loukides, Tim O'Reilly, et al.
1st Edition March 1993
1162 pages (includes CD-ROM)
Random House ISBN 0-679-79073-X

Ideal for UNIX users who hunger for technical—yet accessible—information, *UNIX Power Tools* consists of tips, tricks, concepts, and freeware (CD-ROM included). It also covers add-on utilities and how to take advantage of clever features in the most popular UNIX utilities.

This is a browser's book... like a magazine that you don't read from start to finish, but leaf through repeatedly until you realize that you've read it all. You'll find articles abstracted from O'Reilly Nutshell Handbooks®, new information that highlights program "tricks" and "gotchas," tips posted to the net over the years, and other accumulated wisdom. The goal of *UNIX Power Tools* is to help you think creatively about UNIX and get you to the point where you can analyze your own problems. Your own solutions won't be far behind.

The CD-ROM includes all of the scripts and aliases from the book, plus *perl*, GNU *emacs*, *pbmplus* (manipulation utilities), *ispell*, *screen*, the *sc*spreadsheet, and about 60 other freeware programs. In addition to the source code, all the software is precompiled for Sun3, Sun4, DECstation, IBM RS/6000, HP 9000 (700 series), SCO Xenix, and SCO UNIX. (SCO UNIX binaries will likely also run on other Intel UNIX platforms, including Univel's new UNIXware.)

"Chockful of ideas on how to get the most from UNIX, this book is aimed at those who want to improve their proficiency with this versatile operating system. Best of all, you don't have to be a computer scientist to understand it. If you use UNIX, this book belongs on your desk."
—Book Reviews, *Compuserve Magazine*

"*Unix Power Tools* is an encyclopedic work that belongs next to every serious UNIX user's terminal. If you're already a UNIX wizard, keep this book tucked under your desk for late-night reference when solving those difficult problems."
—Raymond GA Côté, *Byte*

Making T_EX Work

By Norman Walsh
1st Edition April 1994
522 pages, ISBN 1-56592-051-1

TeX is a powerful tool for creating professional-quality typeset text and is unsurpassed at typesetting mathematical equations, scientific text, and multiple languages. Many books describe how you use TeX to construct sentences, paragraphs, and chapters. Until now, no book has described all the software that actually lets you build, run, and use TeX to best advantage on your platform. Because creating a TeX document requires the use of many tools, this lack of information is a serious problem for TeX users.

Making T_EX Work guides you through the maze of tools available in the TeX system. Beyond the core TeX program there are myriad drivers, macro packages, previewers, printing programs, online documentation facilities, graphics programs, and much more. This book describes them all.

The Frame Handbook

By Linda Branagan & Mike Sierra
1st Edition October 1994 (est.)
500 pages (est.), ISBN 1-56592-009-0

A thorough, single-volume guide to using the UNIX version of FrameMaker 4.0, a sophisticated document production system. This book is for everyone who creates technical manuals and reports, from technical writers and editors who will become power users to administrative assistants and engineers. The book contains a thorough introduction to Frame and covers creating document templates, assembling books, and Frame tips and tricks. It begins by discussing the basic features of any text-formatting system: how it handles text and text-based tools (like spell-checking). It quickly gets into areas that benefit from a sophisticated tool like Frame: cross-references and footnotes; styles, master pages, and templates; tables and graphics; tables of contents and indexes; and, for those interested in online access, hypertext. Once you've finished this book, you'll be able to use Frame to create and produce a book or even a series of books.

Exploring Expect

By Don Libes
1st Edition Winter 1994-95 (est.)
500 pages (est.), ISBN 1-56592-090-2

Written by the author of Expect, this is the first book to explain how this new part of the UNIX toolbox can be used to automate *telnet, ftp, passwd, rlogin*, and hundreds of other interactive applications. Based on *Tcl* (Tool Control Language), Expect lets you automate interactive applications that have previously been extremely difficult to handle with any scripting language.

The book briefly describes *Tcl* and how Expect relates to it. It then describes the *Tcl* language, using a combination of reference material and specific, useful examples of its features. It shows how to use Expect in background, in multiple processes, and with standard languages and tools like C, C++, and *Tk*, the X-based extension to *Tcl*. The strength in the book is in its scripts, conveniently listed in a separate index.

"Expect was the first widely used *Tcl* application, and it is still one of the most popular. This is a must-know tool for system administrators and many others."
—John Ousterhout, John.Ousterhout@Eng.Sun.COM

sed & awk

By Dale Dougherty
1st Edition November 1990
414 pages, ISBN 0-937175-59-5

For people who create and modify text files, *sed* and *awk* are power tools for editing. Most of the things that you can do with these programs can be done interactively with a text editor; however, using *sed* and *awk* can save many hours of repetitive work in achieving the same result.

"*sed & awk* is a must for UNIX system programmers and administrators, and even general UNIX readers will benefit. I have over a hundred UNIX and C books in my personal library at home, but only a dozen are duplicated on the shelf where I work. This one just became number twelve."
—*Root Journal*

Learning Perl

By Randal L. Schwartz, Foreword by Larry Wall
1st Edition November 1993
274 pages, ISBN 1-56592-042-2

Learning Perl is ideal for system administrators, programmers, and anyone else wanting a down-to-earth introduction to this useful language. Written by a Perl trainer, its aim is to make a competent, hands-on Perl programmer out of the reader as quickly as possible. The book takes a tutorial approach and includes hundreds of short code examples, along with some lengthy ones. The relatively inexperienced programmer will find *Learning Perl* easily accessible. Each chapter of the book includes practical programming exercises. Solutions are presented for all exercises.

For a comprehensive and detailed guide to advanced programming with Perl, read O'Reilly's companion book, *Programming perl*.

"All-in-all, *Learning Perl* is a fine introductory text that can dramatically ease moving into the world of *perl*. It fills a niche previously filled only by tutorials taught by a small number of *perl* experts.... The UNIX community too often lacks the kind of tutorial that this book offers."
—Rob Kolstad, *;login*

Programming perl

By Larry Wall & Randal L. Schwartz
1st Edition January 1991
482 pages, ISBN 0-937175-64-1

This is the authoritative guide to the hottest new UNIX utility in years, coauthored by its creator, Larry Wall. Perl is a language for easily manipulating text, files, and processes. Perl provides a more concise and readable way to do many jobs that were formerly accomplished (with difficulty) by programming in the C language or one of the shells. *Programming perl* covers Perl syntax, functions, debugging, efficiency, the Perl library, and more, including real-world Perl programs dealing with such issues as system administration and text manipulation. Also includes a pull-out quick-reference card (designed and created by Johan Vromans).

O'Reilly & Associates—
GLOBAL NETWORK NAVIGATOR

The Global Network Navigator (GNN)™ is a unique kind of information service that makes the Internet easy and enjoyable to use. We organize access to the vast information resources of the Internet so that you can find what you want. We also help you understand the Internet and the many ways you can explore it.

In GNN you'll find:

Navigating the Net with GNN

 The *Whole Internet Catalog* contains a descriptive listing of the most useful Net resources and services with live links to those resources.

The *GNN Business Pages* are where you'll learn about companies who have established a presence on the Internet and use its worldwide reach to help educate consumers.

The *Internet Help Desk* helps folks who are new to the Net orient themselves and gets them started on the road to Internet exploration.

News

NetNews is a weekly publication that reports on the news of the Internet, with weekly feature articles that focus on Internet trends and special events. The Sports, Weather, and Comix Pages round out the news.

Special Interest Publications

Whether you're planning a trip or are just interested in reading about the journeys of others, you'll find that the *Travelers' Center* contains a rich collection of feature articles and ongoing columns about travel. In the *Travelers' Center*, you can link to many helpful and informative travel-related Internet resources.

The *Personal Finance Center* is the place to go for information about money management and investment on the Internet. Whether you're an old pro at playing the market or are thinking about investing for the first time, you'll read articles and discover Internet resources that will help you to think of the Internet as a personal finance information tool.

All in all, GNN helps you get more value for the time you spend on the Internet.

 The Best of the Web

GNN received "Honorable Mention" for **"Best Overall Site," "Best Entertainment Service,"** and **"Most Important Service Concept."**

The *GNN NetNews* received "Honorable Mention" for **"Best Document Design."**

Subscribe Today

GNN is available over the Internet as a subscription service. To get complete information about subscribing to GNN, send email to **info@gnn.com**. If you have access to a World Wide Web browser such as Mosaic or Lynx, you can use the following URL to register online: **http://gnn.com/**

If you use a browser that does not support online forms, you can retrieve an email version of the registration form automatically by sending email to **form@gnn.com**. Fill this form out and send it back to us by email, and we will confirm your registration.

O'Reilly on the Net—
ONLINE PROGRAM GUIDE

O'Reilly & Associates offers extensive information through our online resources. If you've got Internet access, we invite you to come and explore our little neck-of-the-woods.

Online Resource Center

Most comprehensive among our online offerings is the O'Reilly Resource Center. Here, you'll find detailed information and descriptions on all O'Reilly products: titles, prices, tables of contents, indexes, author bios, CD-ROM directory listings, reviews... you can even view images of the products themselves. We also supply helpful ordering information: how to contact us, how to order online, distributors and bookstores around the world, discounts, upgrades, etc. In addition, we provide informative literature in the field, featuring articles, interviews, bibliographies, and columns that help you stay informed and abreast.

The Best of the Web

The *O'Reilly Resource Center* was voted "**Best Commercial Site**" by users participating in "Best of the Web '94."

To access ORA's Online Resource Center:

Point your Web browser (e.g., **mosaic** or **lynx**) to:

http://gnn.com/ora/

For the plaintext version, **telnet** or **gopher** to:

gopher.ora.com

(telnetters login: **gopher**)

FTP

The example files and programs in many of our books are available electronically via FTP.

To obtain example files and programs from O'Reilly texts:

ftp to:

ftp.uu.net

cd published/oreilly

or
ftp.ora.com

Ora-news

An easy way to stay informed of the latest projects and products from O'Reilly & Associates is to subscribe to "ora-news," our electronic news service. Subscribers receive email as soon as the information breaks.

To subscribe to "ora-news":

Send email to:
listproc@online.ora.com

and put the following information on the first line of your message (not in "Subject"):
subscribe ora-news "your name" **of** "your company"

For example:
subscribe ora-news Jim Dandy of Mighty Fine Enterprises

Email

Many other helpful customer services are provided via email. Here's a few of the most popular and useful.

Useful email addresses

nuts@ora.com
> For general questions and information.

bookquestions@ora.com
> For technical questions, or corrections, concerning book contents.

order@ora.com
> To order books online and for ordering questions.

catalog@ora.com
> To receive a free copy of our magazine/catalog, "ora.com" (please include a snailmail address).

Snailmail and phones

O'Reilly & Associates, Inc.
103A Morris Street, Sebastopol, CA 95472
Inquiries: **707-829-0515, 800-998-9938**
Credit card orders: **800-889-8969**
FAX: **707-829-0104**

O'Reilly & Associates—
LISTING OF TITLES

INTERNET

!%@:: A Directory of Electronic Mail
    Addressing & Networks
Connecting to the Internet: An O'Reilly Buyer's Guide
Internet In A Box
MH & xmh: E-mail for Users & Programmers
The Mosaic Handbook for Microsoft Windows
The Mosaic Handbook for the Macintosh
The Mosaic Handbook for the X Window System
Smileys
The Whole Internet User's Guide & Catalog

SYSTEM ADMINISTRATION

Computer Security Basics
DNS and BIND
Essential System Administration
Linux Network Administrator's Guide (Fall 94 est.)
Managing Internet Information Services (Fall 94 est.)
Managing NFS and NIS
Managing UUCP and Usenet
sendmail
Practical UNIX Security
PGP: Pretty Good Privacy (Winter 94/95 est.)
System Performance Tuning
TCP/IP Network Administration
termcap & terminfo
X Window System Administrator's Guide: Volume 8
X Window System ,R6, Companion CD (Fall 94 est.)

USING UNIX AND X

BASICS

Learning GNU Emacs
Learning the Korn Shell
Learning the UNIX Operating System
Learning the vi Editor
SCO UNIX in a Nutshell
The USENET Handbook (Winter 94/95 est.)
Using UUCP and Usenet
UNIX in a Nutshell: System V Edition
The X Window System in a Nutshell
X Window System User's Guide: Volume 3
X Window System User's Guide, Motif Ed.: Vol. 3M
X User Tools (with CD-ROM) (10/94 est.)

ADVANCED

Exploring Expect (Winter 94/95 est.)
The Frame Handbook (10/94 est.)
Making TeX Work
Learning Perl
Programming perl
sed & awk
UNIX Power Tools (with CD-ROM)

PROGRAMMING UNIX, C, AND MULTI-PLATFORM

FORTRAN/SCIENTIFIC COMPUTING

High Performance Computing
Migrating to Fortran 90
UNIX for FORTRAN Programmers

C PROGRAMMING LIBRARIES

Practical C Programming
POSIX Programmer's Guide
POSIX.4: Programming for the Real World
    (Fall 94 est.)
Programming with curses
Understanding and Using COFF
Using C on the UNIX System

C PROGRAMMING TOOLS

Checking C Programs with lint
lex & yacc
Managing Projects with make
Power Programming with RPC
Software Portability with imake

MULTI-PLATFORM PROGRAMMING

Encyclopedia of Graphics File Formats
Distributing Applications Across DCE and
    Windows NT
Guide to Writing DCE Applications
Multi-Platform Code Management
Understanding DCE
Understanding Japanese Information Processing
ORACLE Performance Tuning

BERKELEY 4.4 SOFTWARE DISTRIBUTION

4.4BSD System Manager's Manual
4.4BSD User's Reference Manual
4.4BSD User's Supplementary Documents
4.4BSD Programmer's Reference Manual
4.4BSD Programmer's Supplementary Documents
4.4BSD-Lite CD Companion
4.4BSD-Lite CD Companion: International Version

X PROGRAMMING

Motif Programming Manual: Volume 6A
Motif Reference Manual: Volume 6B
Motif Tools
PEXlib Programming Manual
PEXlib Reference Manual
PHIGS Programming Manual (soft or hard cover)
PHIGS Reference Manual
Programmer's Supplement for R6 (Winter 94/95 est.)
Xlib Programming Manual: Volume 1
Xlib Reference Manual: Volume 2
X Protocol Reference Manual, R5: Volume 0
X Protocol Reference Manual, R6: Volume 0 (11/94 est.)
X Toolkit Intrinsics Programming Manual: Vol. 4
X Toolkit Intrinsics Programming Manual,
    Motif Edition: Volume 4M
X Toolkit Intrinsics Reference Manual: Volume 5
XView Programming Manual: Volume 7A
XView Reference Manual: Volume 7B

THE X RESOURCE

A QUARTERLY WORKING JOURNAL FOR X PROGRAMMERS

The X Resource: Issues 0 through 12
    (Issue 12 available 10/94)

BUSINESS/CAREER

Building a Successful Software Business
Love Your Job!

TRAVEL

Travelers' Tales Thailand
Travelers' Tales Mexico
Travelers' Tales India (Winter 94/95 est.)

AUDIOTAPES

INTERNET TALK RADIO'S "GEEK OF THE WEEK" INTERVIEWS

The Future of the Internet Protocol, 4 hours
Global Network Operations, 2 hours
Mobile IP Networking, 1 hour
Networked Information and
    Online Libraries, 1 hour
Security and Networks, 1 hour
European Networking, 1 hour

NOTABLE SPEECHES OF THE INFORMATION AGE

John Perry Barlow, 1.5 hours

O'Reilly & Associates—
INTERNATIONAL DISTRIBUTORS

Customers outside North America can now order O'Reilly & Associates books through the following distributors. They offer our international customers faster order processing, more bookstores, increased representation at tradeshows worldwide, and the high quality, responsive service our customers have come to expect.

EUROPE, MIDDLE EAST, AND AFRICA
(except Germany, Switzerland, and Austria)

INQUIRIES
International Thomson Publishing Europe
Berkshire House
168-173 High Holborn
London WC1V 7AA
United Kingdom
Telephone: 44-71-497-1422
Fax: 44-71-497-1426
Email: ora.orders@itpuk.co.uk

ORDERS
International Thomson Publishing Services, Ltd.
Cheriton House, North Way
Andover, Hampshire SP10 5BE
United Kingdom
Telephone: 44-264-342-832 (UK orders)
Telephone: 44-264-342-806 (outside UK)
Fax: 44-264-364418 (UK orders)
Fax: 44-264-342761 (outside UK)

GERMANY, SWITZERLAND, AND AUSTRIA
International Thomson Publishing GmbH
O'Reilly-International Thomson Verlag
Attn: Mr. G. Miske
Königswinterer Strasse 418
53227 Bonn
Germany
Telephone: 49-228-970240
Fax: 49-228-441342
Email: gerd@orade.ora.com

THE AMERICAS, JAPAN, AND OCEANIA
O'Reilly & Associates, Inc.
103A Morris Street
Sebastopol, CA 95472 U.S.A.
Telephone: 707-829-0515
Telephone: 800-998-9938 (U.S. & Canada)
Fax: 707-829-0104
Email: order@ora.com

ASIA
(except Japan)

INQUIRIES
International Thomson Publishing Asia
221 Henderson Road
#05 10 Henderson Building
Singapore 0315
Telephone: 65-272-6496
Fax: 65-272-6498

ORDERS
Telephone: 65-268-7867
Fax: 65-268-6727

AUSTRALIA
WoodsLane Pty. Ltd.
Unit 8, 101 Darley Street (P.O. Box 935)
Mona Vale NSW 2103
Australia
Telephone: 61-2-979-5944
Fax: 61-2-997-3348
Email: woods@tmx.mhs.oz.au

NEW ZEALAND
WoodsLane New Zealand Ltd.
21 Cooks Street (P.O. Box 575)
Wanganui, New Zealand
Telephone: 64-6-347-6543
Fax: 64-6-345-4840
Email: woods@tmx.mhs.oz.au